FROM BABYLON TO BETHLEHEM

From
BABYLON TO BETHLEHEM

*The Story of the Jews for the
last Five Centuries before Christ*

BY

LAURENCE E. BROWNE, D.D.
Professor of Theology, University of Leeds

Revised and enlarged with the
assistance of

MATTHEW BLACK, D.Litt.
Lecturer in New Testament, University of Leeds

CAMBRIDGE
W. HEFFER & SONS LIMITED
1951

First Published - - - - 1926

Reprinted - - - - - 1937

Second Edition - - - - 1951

Printed in Great Britain at the Works of
W. HEFFER AND SONS LTD., CAMBRIDGE, ENGLAND

Contents

v

Preface

THIS book was originally written at the request of the late Dr. V. S. Azariah, Bishop of Dornakal, for the use of his clergy. It was first published in English in 1926 by Messrs W. Heffer & Sons, Ltd., who kindly allowed it to be published in Telugu by the Christian Literature Society for India (Madras) in 1932, and in Chinese by the Christian Literature Society (Shanghai) in 1935. It was reprinted in English in 1936.

Now, having been out of print since 1943, it has been thoroughly revised and enlarged for a second edition. Experience of several examinations, for which it has been used as a text-book, has shown that students have difficulty in obtaining and using the large amount of Jewish non-canonical literature of the period. The standard English edition of this literature is the two large volumes edited by Dr. Charles entitled *Apocrypha and Pseudepigrapha*, and there are also handy volumes of translations of the separate books published by S.P.C.K. in the series *Translations of Early Documents*. As many school libraries do not possess these works, it was decided to include in this new edition a larger number of quotations. For permission to quote from Dr. Charles' volumes I am greatly indebted to the Oxford University Press. Both in choosing the new illustrative passages, and in their interpretation, I have been greatly helped by my colleague Dr. Matthew Black. In fact, so great is the importance of some of the passages relating to the development of the Messianic hope to which he has drawn my attention, that it is only right that his name should appear on the title page.

For the further study of the earlier part of the period advanced students are referred to my *Early Judaism*, where evidence is given for some of the statements here made. Other books which students will find helpful are Dr. Edwyn Bevan's *Jerusalem under the High Priests*, and Dr. Norman Snaith's new book *The Jews from Cyrus to Herod*, which was published earlier this year.

L. E. B.

LEEDS, *September*, 1950.

Chapter I

THE JEWS IN EXILE

BEFORE 538 B.C.

At the time when our story opens the Jews were still in exile in Babylonia. Some forty years or rather more had elapsed since their fathers and mothers, heavily weighted with chains, had been driven and dragged by Nebuchadnezzar's rough soldiery from their mountain home in Judah and set to forced labour in the plains of Babylon. The bitterness of that enslavement had never been forgotten, though now the children were free men earning a comfortable living as traders and money-lenders and sometimes as successful merchants. Babylonia in those days was a very fertile land, made fertile by canals and channels, which men had constructed to lead the waters of the great Euphrates and Tigris rivers over the fields of crops. And that fertility brought wealth and prosperity, not only to the men who tilled the soil but to everyone in the land, even the Jewish pedlar or money-lender. Contrast the lot of these Jews in Babylonia, with that of their countrymen left behind on the barren hills of Judaea. With a few half-starved flocks and herds they wandered from hill to hill trying to find pasture. Sometimes they would scratch the stony surface of the ground and sow a little corn, but the chances were that at harvest time there would be a sudden raid of Moabites or Edomites, and the helpless Jews would see the fruit of their labours carried away before their eyes. So insecure was their tenure of the land that a man rarely lived to eat the fruit of fig or vine or olive which he had planted. Comparing the lot of the Palestinian and the Babylonian Jews, all the advantage seemed to lie with the latter. All that wealth and prosperity could give was theirs and was denied their Judaean cousins. But one thing outweighed all the advantages, and that was that the old edict of Nebuchadnezzar forbidding the Jews to return to their mountain home had never been repealed. Living prosperously in a land of plenty they could never forget their home-land, and to their thirsty hearts the land of exile seemed like a barren, sandy desert. It was worse than being in the middle of the Sahara, because the desert was within their hearts instead of under their feet.

"By the rivers of Babylon,
There we sat down, yea, we wept,
When we remembered Zion.
Upon the willows in the midst thereof
We hanged up our harps.
For there they that led us captive required of us songs,
And they that wasted us required of us mirth, saying,
Sing us one of the songs of Zion.
How shall we sing the Lord's song
In a strange land?
If I forget thee, O Jerusalem,
Let my right hand forget her cunning.
Let my tongue cleave to the roof of my mouth,
If I remember thee not;
If I prefer not Jerusalem
Above my chief joy" (Ps. cxxxvii. 1–6).

Such was the frame of mind of the Jews when

some news of the outer world began to trickle in, giving them a start of joyous surprise as when a traveller in the desert comes by chance upon a wady and finds a little ooze of water in its rocky bed. There were no newspapers in Babylon in those days, and news is always more exciting where there are no newspapers. When you read a thing in the newspaper you generally believe it at once, and scarcely stop to ask where the story came from. But bazaar talk is different. When you hear it you smile and say, "It's only a rumour of the bazaar." No one can tell you where it came from. The old fruit-seller told it, and he has forgotten who told him. A few days later others are telling the same thing. Yet a few days more and all the world knows it; and still no one knows who brought the news. And so it was that the talk began in the bazaars of Babylon about Cyrus. First they only heard tell of an upstart prince named Cyrus, who was supposed to have won a kingdom; whether it was history or fiction they neither knew nor cared —it was a pretty story. Then details were added, and, no sooner was it generally agreed that he must be a real person, than the news came that Persia and Media had become united as one empire, with Cyrus as their king. This was soon confirmed on unimpeachable authority. But still the rumours of the bazaar kept ahead of history, and the most fantastic stories were told of the exploits of the conqueror, some of which were falsified and some confirmed when authentic news came through. Westwards and northwards he marched, and everyone knew the prize that he was making for,

for they had all heard the fame of Croesus, king of Lydia, the wealthiest man the world had ever known. Excitement in the bazaar grew intense, as men watched two reckless gamblers. One day rumour had it that the wealth of Croesus had fallen into the hands of Cyrus. Next day it was contradicted by a rumour that the Lydian army had overthrown the invader. So with bated breath the Babylonians watched and waited as rumour followed rumour, till the news came from eye-witnesses, who had seen the Persian army returning, and had seen armed guards convoying carts heaped with vessels of gold. The famous oracle at Delphi had played a grim joke on Croesus, for when he enquired of the oracle he was told that if he advanced against Cyrus, he would destroy a great kingdom; but the oracle omitted to tell him that the kingdom to be destroyed would be his own. With the conquest of Lydia, Cyrus was master of all the lands stretching from what is now Afghanistan in the east to the coast of Asia Minor in the west. Eager for new lands to conquer, and greedy for more booty, he naturally turned towards the valleys of the Euphrates and Tigris, which, together with Syria and Palestine formed the Babylonian Empire. No one in Babylonia seriously expected to beat the conqueror of Croesus, for weaklings had succeeded the great Nebuchadnezzar, and the people waited with a kind of hopeless fatalism for the day when the foreigners should overrun their land. Those were days of unrelieved gloom for the Babylonians, and, if there had been anywhere to flee to, many of them would have fled.

It will be remembered that Nebuchadnezzar had adopted the policy of transporting large numbers of the population of the countries he had conquered. Not only Jews, but many others, had been brought into Babylonia. At the time the policy was successful, for it weakened the subject kingdoms, but after Nebuchadnezzar's death the folly of it was seen when Babylonia had a large discontented foreign population. So long as there was no external enemy, these foreign residents in Babylon could do little harm; but they were obviously a great menace to the empire when Cyrus was proceeding to attack. Naturally they would rise to join the invader, who would be sure to reverse the policy of Nebuchadnezzar and let them return to their old homes. And among those who were prepared to welcome Cyrus as their coming deliverer were the Jews. Anyone with any political foresight would have said that as soon as Cyrus conquered Babylon he would permit the exiles to return, if they wished, to their own lands; the Jews would no longer feel the sting of being in exile, and they would continue to live in Babylonia as prosperous residents, and certainly would not return to the poverty-stricken land of Judaea which they called their home. But in real history, as in novels, the unexpected often happens. If the unexpected had not happened this history would never have been written.

The unexpected course of events was due to one man, a man so great that he changed the course of Jewish history. If he had had a more responsive audience he would have changed the whole history of the world. It is a curious thing that we do not

know the name of this great man. No hint of his
personal history has reached us. The man himself
seems to have been swallowed up in his message.
The words he wrote, together with the writings of
Isaiah and of several other prophets, have been
put together in one book under the title of "Isaiah."
Chapters xl. to lv. (with the exception of xlix. 14—
l. 3) are the work of this great prophet of the exile,
and for lack of his real name we generally refer
to him as Second Isaiah.

The words with which Second Isaiah's prophecy
opened doubtless gained for him an immediate
hearing, for he declared the coming deliverance
that all the Jews were expecting.

> "Comfort ye, comfort ye my people, saith your God.
> Speak ye comfortably to Jerusalem, and cry unto her,
> that her warfare is accomplished, that her iniquity is
> pardoned; that she hath received of the Lord's hand
> double for all her sins" (Isa. xl. 1–2).

Only, while others were thinking in terms of
politics, Second Isaiah spoke of moral values.
The exile had been Israel's punishment for sin, the
punishment had been excessive, the sin was wiped
out, the release was due, and the Lord would grant
it. The return of Israel to Judaea was to be no
shamefaced sneaking homeward, but a triumphal
march with Yahweh at the head of His host.

> "The voice of one that crieth, Prepare ye in the
> wilderness the way of the Lord, make straight in the
> desert a highway for our God. Every valley shall be
> exalted, and every mountain and hill shall be made low:
> and the crooked shall be made straight, and the rough
> places plain: and the glory of the Lord shall be revealed,

and all flesh shall see it together: for the mouth of the Lord hath spoken it" (Isa. xl. 3–5).

Now the Jew was very keen about his religion: he knew it was immeasurably superior to everybody else's religion: but he was much more attracted by the glamour attached to it than by its obligations to moral conduct. And so, though he could not perhaps easily appreciate the moral conditions necessary for release from exile, he could thoroughly enjoy the prospect of a religious triumph of the Ancestral God. Second Isaiah had the poet's art to choose expressions that would raise an immediate response from his hearers, and a poet's soul to put his thoughts in such language that even in translation it is of incomparable beauty. But, being more than a poet, he could not stay content with delineating, even in the sublimest language, those crabbed and tribal notions of Yahweh, which were current among his fellow Jews. It was impossible for them to realise the meaning of their deliverance till they could see it in relation to God's purposes; and they could not understand God's purposes until their conception of God was widened.

Since the days of Isaiah, two hundred years earlier, the Jews had been familiar with the teaching that Yahweh was the only God. To have the only God as their tribal deity was flattering to themselves, and they therefore had no hesitation in believing it, without for a moment thinking out the logical consequences of the belief. Second Isaiah did not blame them for this, but led them on step by step from what they knew of God to what they ought to know.

"Who hath measured the waters in the hollow of His
hand, and meted out heaven with the span, and com-
prehended the dust of the earth in a measure, and
weighed the mountains in scales, and the hills in a
balance? Who hath directed the spirit of the Lord, or
being His counseller hath taught Him? With whom
took He counsel, and who instructed Him, and taught
Him in the path of judgment, and taught Him knowledge, and showed to Him the way of understanding?"
(Isa. xl. 12–14).

One thing especially marked off Yahweh from other
gods, that of Him alone no idols were made. Ever
since the days of Solomon at least, He had been
worshipped without an idol.* In the temple of
Jerusalem He was thought of as seated unseen on
the cherubim, which were probably winged sphinxes.
In the temple of Bethel we are told by the Judaean
writers that He was represented by an idol like a bull.
It may well be that the bull was popularly regarded
as an idol of Yahweh, but there seems some reason
for thinking that in Bethel too the original intention
may have been to worship Him as seated unseen on
His animal vehicle. In any case, the bull of Bethel
had been destroyed more than a century before
Second Isaiah's time. This superiority of Yahweh-
worship gave Second Isaiah a text, so to speak, from
which to begin his sermon on the attributes of
Yahweh.

"To whom then will ye liken God? or what likeness will
ye compare unto Him? The graven image, a workman
melted it, and the goldsmith spreadeth it over with gold,
and casteth for it silver chains" (Isa. xl. 18–19).

* There is no evidence for the suggestion that the brazen
serpent (2 Kings xviii. 4) was an idol of Yahweh.

We are not to suppose that the violent attacks on idolatry were intended to convert the Babylonians. The sarcastic humour would only have irritated any idolaters who heard it, but it was well calculated to deepen the Jew's impression that Yahweh alone lived and ruled, and the gods of the other nations were lifeless phantoms of the brain. Could anyone have found a more telling way of describing the fatherly care of Yahweh, than in the comparison of the idols of Bel and Nebo carried as a burden on the weary beasts with the living God bearing His people as His burden?

"Bel boweth down, Nebo stoopeth; their idols are upon the beasts, and upon the cattle; the things that ye carried about are made a load, a burden to the weary beast. They stoop, they bow down together; they could not deliver the burden, but themselves are gone into captivity. Hearken unto me, O house of Jacob, and all the remnant of the house of Israel, which have been borne by me from the belly, which have been carried from the womb; and even to old age I am He, and even to hoar hairs will I carry you: I have made, and I will bear; yea, I will carry, and will deliver. To whom will ye liken me, and make me equal, and compare me, that we may be like?" (Isa. xlvi. 1–5).

From Yahweh's position as the only existing God it follows that He must control the history of all the nations. It used to be thought that Marduk controlled the destines of Babylonia, Chemosh the destinies of Ammon, and Yahweh the destinies of Israel. But since these other gods are now declared to be non-existent, it must follow that all their functions are exercised by Yahweh. And moreover, since Yahweh is known to be a holy God, He not only controls the history of the world, but controls it well. The prophet challenged the idols to show in what way they can control history, either by foretelling the future or by explaining the past.

> "Produce your case, saith the Lord; bring forth your strong reasons, saith the King of Jacob. Let them bring them forth, and declare unto us what shall happen: declare ye the former things, what they be, that we may consider them, and know the latter end of them; or show us things for to come. Declare the things that are to come hereafter, that we may know that ye are gods: yea, do good, or do evil, that we may be dismayed, and behold it together. Behold, ye are of nothing, and your work of naught; an abomination is he that chooseth you" (Isa. xli. 21–24).

The challenge is unanswered, for it is Yahweh alone who controls history.

> "Who hath raised up one from the east at whose foot victory attends? (Isa. xli. 2).

> "I have raised up one from the north, and he is come; from the rising of the sun one that calleth upon my name" (Isa. xli. 25).

> "I am the Lord, that maketh all things; that stretcheth forth the heavens alone; that spreadeth abroad the earth; who is with me? that frustrateth the tokens of the liars, and maketh diviners mad; that turneth wise men backward, and maketh their knowledge foolish; that confirmeth the word of His servant, and performeth the counsel of His messengers; that saith of Jerusalem, she shall be inhabited; and of the cities of Judah, They shall be built, and I will raise up the waste places thereof; that saith to the deep, Be dry, and I will dry up thy rivers; that saith of Cyrus, He is my shepherd, and shall perform all my pleasure" (Isa. xliv. 24–28).

The last passage claims the definite fulfilment of a prophecy: by bringing about the restoration of

Israel, Yahweh was confirming the word of His servant Jeremiah.

> "Thus saith the Lord, After seventy years be accomplished for Babylon I will visit you, and perform my good word toward you, in causing you to return to this place" (Jer. xxix. 10).

There is something amazingly bold in the claim of Second Isaiah. Everyone knew that love of gold and lust for power were the motives that led Cyrus on his march; everyone knew that he was a polytheist and idolater, and had probably never heard so much as the name of Yahweh. He was not even, like Darius I and the kings that succeeded him, a follower of Zoroaster, who had taught men to worship one good God. But Second Isaiah brushed aside all those immediate causes, for underneath it all he could see the guiding hand of Providence who could even turn the wrath of man to His praise. So the prophet represents Yahweh as saying to Cyrus:—

> "For Jacob my servant's sake, and Israel my chosen, I have called thee by thy name: I have surnamed thee, though thou hast not known me" (Isa. xlv. 4).

We can imagine the prophet meditating on these world movements, on armies marching to far distant cities, on empires rising and falling. We can imagine him wondering what purpose was being worked out by the great God who sat aloft and controlled it all. And first there came to his mind—for he was a Jew—the effect it would have on the Jews, how the race now scattered and exiled, despondent and leaderless, should be restored to be an independent kingdom as in ancient days, with a temple at

Jerusalem. For a Jew it was a great vision to see Jerusalem restored to the fabulous golden magnificence of Solomon's days. And yet—the prophet thought again—truly a glorious vision for a Jew; but is Yahweh a Jew, that all the forces of the nations should be bent to magnify Jerusalem and Judaism? The Jewish soul within the prophet struggled to hold down the truth, but the full human soul within him burst the bands and triumphed. The certainty possessed him that the purpose of the world's God was world-wide. The wealth of Croesus and of Babylon, the security of empires, were being thrown away as things of little value. Such expenditure was too great to be accounted for as the price paid for the advantage of the Jews alone. It could only be accounted for as part of a wider purpose of giving to the nations the gift of God Himself, of giving to God the homage and devotion of His creatures. It seemed so clear when he began to think about it, that since God had made all men of every race, He must want all of them to know and serve Him, and not only the Jews. And then the prophet hesitated again; for how could the conquest of Cyrus bring the world to God? Surely the proud conqueror would not sit at the feet of Jewish teachers and learn of them? No, it must be by the mighty hand of God. Then would God suddenly overthrow Cyrus so as to show His power? That would not do, for it would only make Him seem like Cyrus and Croesus and Nebuchadnezzar and all the world's rich men and conquerors. No, God must show, not His might, but His character; and now, at length, the prophet saw how the character of God would be shown. God had promised to save Israel, and so long as Israel was scattered, God's promises seemed to delay fulfilment; but if Israel was restored, all the world would know that God was true to His promise. That was the demonstration of His character, which God was preparing. Looking back, the prophet saw in this more than the explanation of Persian history. It explained that affliction which had befallen Israel, apparently so incommensurate with her sins, as an earlier poet of the exile had lamented—

"Behold, and see if there is any sorrow like unto my sorrow, which is done unto me!" (Lam. i. 12).

And as the prophet meditated on the sufferings of Israel he caught some glimpse of that great mystery, which to later generations was made known by the cross of Calvary, that if you would help others you must suffer for them. The miserable suffering of a malefactor was the due reward of his deeds, but the suffering of one who served others by his pains was a glorious thing brightening a dark world. It is the combination in Second Isaiah of the two ideas of suffering and service that exalts service and lifts the burden of suffering. The Suffering Servant, by bearing the limit of pain, holds back nothing in his devotion of himself for others.

"The Lord God hath given me the tongue of them that
    are taught,
  That I should know how to sustain the weary with words.
  The Lord God hath opened mine ear,
  In the morning He wakeneth mine ear to hear as they
    that are taught.
  I was not rebellious, nor turned away backwards.

I gave my back to the smiters, and my cheeks to them
    that plucked off the hair.
I hid not my face from shame and spitting.
For the Lord God will help me;
Therefore have I not been confounded" (Isa. l. 4–7).

"Surely he hath borne our griefs, and carried our sorrows;
    Yet we did esteem him stricken, smitten of God and
    afflicted.
But he was wounded for our transgressions,
He was bruised for our iniquities,
The chastisement of our peace was upon him,
And with his stripes we are healed.
All we like sheep have gone astray;
We have turned every one to his own way;
And the Lord hath laid on him the iniquity of us all"
    (Isa. liii. 4–6).

Such passages as these that speak of the ideal
Suffering Servant have never found complete
fulfilment save in One, and Christian interpreters
have therefore been fully justified in treating them
as prophecies of our Lord Jesus Christ. But Second
Isaiah was not concerned with impossible ideals, or
ideals only to be fulfilled in another age than his.
His hope, as we have seen, was that Israel's sufferings might be used in service, so that the great
doings of those days might work out the purpose of
God for humanity. The prophet felt deeply enough
the difficulty, that Israel was unworthy to play such
a part.

"Who is blind, but my servant? or deaf, as my
    messenger that I send?" (Isa. xlii. 19).

But sinful though Israel has been, the prophet can
look on the sin as past and atoned for. God had
made Israel for this purpose, and in using Israel as
His agent will show His power.

"Remember these things, O Jacob; and Israel for thou
art my servant.

I have formed thee; thou art my servant. O Israel,
thou shalt not be forgotten of me.

I have blotted out as a thick cloud thy transgressions,
and as a cloud thy sins.

Return unto me, for I have redeemed thee.

Sing, O ye heavens, for the Lord hath done it; shout ye
lower parts of the earth.

Break forth into singing, ye mountains, O forest, and
every tree therein.

For the Lord hath redeemed Jacob, and will glorify
Himself in Israel" (Isa. xliv. 21–23).

The task of Israel the Lord's servant cannot stop
at the restoration of the nation of Israel, but must
include the Gentiles in its scope.

"It is too light a thing that thou shouldest be my servant
to raise up the tribes of Jacob,

And to restore the preserved of Israel. I will also give
thee for a light to the Gentiles,

That thou mayest be my salvation unto the end of the
earth" (Isa. xlix. 6).

"Behold my servant, whom I uphold,

My chosen in whom my soul delighteth.

I have put my spirit upon him;

He shall bring forth judgment to the Gentiles"
(Isa. xlii. 1).

"Incline your ear, and come unto me;

Hear and your soul shall live:

And I will make an everlasting covenant with you
(i.e. Israel),

Even the mercies made sure to David.

Behold, I have given him (i.e. David) for a witness to the
peoples,

A leader and commander to the peoples.

Behold, thou (i.e. Israel) shalt call a nation that thou
knowest not,

And a nation that knew not thee shall run unto thee

> Because of the Lord thy God,
> And for the Holy One of Israel,
> For He hath glorified thee" (Isa. lv. 3–5).

> "The Lord hath made bare His holy arm in the eyes of all
>   the nations;
> And all the ends of the earth shall see the salvation of
>   our God" (Isa. lii. 10).

Second Isaiah did not think of Israelites going out as missionary preachers in the modern sense:

> "He shall not cry nor lift up,
> Nor make his voice to be heard in the street.
> A bruised reed shall he not break,
> And smoking flax shall he not quench" (Isa. xlii. 2).

But an opportunity would arise for Israel to give its witness in words when Gentiles come to seek the true religion—

> "They shall fall down unto thee,
> They shall make supplication unto thee,
> Saying, Surely God is in thee" (Isa. xlv. 14).

That then was Second Isaiah's reading of history. He saw the politics of the nations as a game of chess. The hand that moved the pieces was the unseen hand of God; one of those pieces, unlike the others, was not passive in the hand of God, but was consciously and actively setting itself to serve His purpose and work out His plan. Israel, the Servant of the Lord, was by his self-devotion to be the chief instrument in the world's salvation.

One would have thought that it was obvious that Second Isaiah, as a great preacher, was speaking to his congregation, and was not lifting up his head and speaking to the roof. But many commentators have forgotten this, and have landed themselves into endless difficulties by denying the plain statement that the Servant of the Lord meant Israel. Even though the prophecy fits Jesus Christ better than it ever fitted the Israelites, it was the latter to whom he was speaking, in order to encourage them to take the path of self-sacrificing service. It is true, however, that the picture seems to be that of an individual; and the explanation is that already in Jewish thought there was one individual who represented the nation. That was the Messiah; and in lv. 3–5, quoted above, the prophet identifies this Messiah both with the nation and with the Suffering Servant. Starting with a reminiscence of God's promise to David (2 Sam. vii. 15–16), the prophet sees it fulfilled both in "David," i.e. in the Davidic Messianic king of the future, and also in the nation of Israel; and both are represented as carrying out the task allotted to the Servant of the Lord. Thus the identification of the Servant with the Messiah and with the nation is established. Another passage linking these various ideas is Isa. lxv. 9, where the population of the future nation to spring from Jacob (i.e. northern Israel) and Judah is called "my chosen" and "my servants." Though the conception of the Servant was not much favoured by later Jewish thought,* the thought of the Messiah as both an individual, and also as the personified nation, was never forgotten, and needs to be remembered by us if we are to understand the later Messianic passages.

NOTE.

On this chapter read Isaiah xl–lv. (omitting xlix. 14–l. 3).

* But see Test. Levi xviii. 6, quoted below on page 95f.

Chapter II

HOW THEY BUILT THE TEMPLE

520 B.C.

IN reading past history, we often have records of the words and deeds of great men, and nothing at all about the common people. But of course it is the common people who are the most important, and great men are only important if they can help and guide the rest of the people. We should make a great mistake if we judged history only by the men of note. Our first chapter was concerned very largely with the words of Second Isaiah. What is really important in the history of the Jews is to know the influence of Second Isaiah on the nation as a whole. And seeing that till the coming of Jesus Christ no prophet arose to be compared with Second Isaiah, we shall find the teaching of Second Isaiah a useful standard by which to judge the Jews in the succeeding periods of these five centuries B.C. No continuous history of the period from 500 B.C. to the Christian era can be written, either of the rulers and their wars, or of the more important life and customs of the people; but from time to time the curtain lifts and shows some glimpse of what was going on.

When Cyrus eventually came and conquered Babylon in 538 B.C. he gave permission for all the subject peoples to return to their own lands and take their gods with them. Here was the opportunity of the Jews to hasten to Judaea; and we gaze impatiently as the curtain rises to see what they did. History is perfectly clear that they simply did nothing. That of course is very disappointing to us, if we expected that the whole nation was going to respond to the call of Second Isaiah. It was also very disappointing to later Jews, who thought that their ancestors must have taken the first opportunity to return to Jerusalem and rebuild the temple. In fact, the author of the book of Ezra, who lived two centuries later, was so convinced that his ancestors must have done so that he could only suppose the historians had forgotten to record it. And so in the first three chapters of Ezra we read an account of how the Jews returned to Jerusalem under Sheshbazzar in the first year of Cyrus, and in the following year laid the foundation of the temple. But the author was carried away by his feeling of what ought to have happened; for it is perfectly clear from the book of Haggai that there was no considerable return of Jews nor any foundation of the temple till eighteen years had elapsed since the advent of Cyrus. Disappointing as this fact may be to us who reverence the prophets, it is a fact that we must clearly grasp that the immediate effect of Second Isaiah's preaching was nil. Apart from any of his nobler ideas, the Jews did not even follow his advice to return to their native land:—

"Go ye forth of Babylon, flee ye from the Chaldeans" (Isa. xlviii. 20).

It is not of course to be denied that some few people may have returned to Judaea. Indeed it is

probable that it was the return of a few men of
energy, which inspired the inhabitants of Judaea
to take heart and build the temple. Four names
are specially connected with the enterprise: Haggai
and Zechariah were prophets who urged that it
should be undertaken; Zerubbabel was the Governor;
and Jeshua the High Priest. Whether any of these
four were born in Babylonia we do not know—
Zerubbabel's name certainly suggests some con-
nection with Babel, i.e. Babylon—but the people
whom Haggai addressed were men born in the
land, and not returned exiles.

It was in the year 520 B.C., a year after Darius I
had succeeded to the Persian throne, that Haggai
began to urge the building of the temple. The
people said the time had not come for such an
enterprise, to which he gave the incontrovertible
reply that they were living themselves in nicely
panelled houses. He said their poverty was due
to the temple being in ruins. He said,

"Go up to the mountain, and bring wood, and build
the house; and I will take pleasure in it, and I will be
glorified, saith Yahweh. Ye looked for much, and,
lo, it came to little; and when ye brought it home, I blew
upon it. Why? saith Yahweh Sabaoth. Because of my
house that lieth waste, while ye run every man to his
own house. Therefore on account of you the heavens
withhold their dew, and the earth withholds her fruit.
And I called for a drought upon the land, and upon the
mountains, and upon the corn, and upon the wine, and
upon the oil, and upon that which the ground bringeth
forth, and upon men, and upon cattle, and upon all the
labour of the hands. And now consider, I pray you, from
this day and onwards, from before the laying of one
stone upon another in the temple of Yahweh, how ye

fare. One cometh to a heap of twenty measures, and there are ten; one cometh to the wine vat to draw fifty vessels, and there are twenty. Consider: Is the grain still in the barn? Moreover the vine, the fig-tree, the pomegranates and the olive tree have not yet borne fruit. From this day will I bless" (Hag. i. 8–11, ii. 15–19).

It must be admitted that the appeal to build the temple in order to get good crops was not on the highest level, though even Christians sometimes find it hard to work for the glory of God without seeking a reward. Men of the type of Haggai work for immediate results and get them, and are impatient of the methods of really great spiritual geniuses like Second Isaiah, who may achieve little or nothing in their lifetime, but hold out ideals which are the inspiration of future generations. The effect of Haggai's sermon was immediate: within less than a month the work had actually begun under the leadership of Zerubbabel and Jeshua, and with the hearty co-operation of all the people. The only thing that at all held them back was the fear that the new temple would not approach the magnificence of Solomon's temple; so after the building had been proceeding for about a month Haggai encouraged them by saying,

"Who is left among you that saw this house in its former glory? and how do ye see it now? is it not in your eyes as nothing? Yet now be strong, O Zerubbabel, saith Yahweh; and be strong, O Joshua, son of Jehozadak, the high priest; and be strong, all ye people of the land, saith Yahweh, and work; for I am with you, saith Yahweh Sabaoth. . . . The latter glory of this house shall be greater than the former, saith Yahweh Sabaoth; and in this place will I give peace, saith Yahweh Sabaoth" (Hag. ii. 3–4, 9).

It was soon after this sermon that Zechariah decided to throw his weight on the same side. His first sermon, "Thus saith the Lord of Hosts, return unto me, and I will return unto you," was certain to be agreeably received by his audience, who, by their efforts in building, were already doing what he asked them to do.

At this juncture an incident occurred which gave the Jews the opportunity for magnanimity, which Second Isaiah had hoped for. It was one of those opportunities of which J. Russell Lowell speaks in his hymn—

> "Once to every man and nation
>   Comes the moment to decide,
> In the strife of truth with falsehood,
>   For the good or evil side;
>
>   .   .   .   .
>
> And the choice goes by for ever
>   'Twixt that darkness and that light"
>   (*English Hymnal*, 563).

The Samaritans came and asked the Jews whether they might join in the work of building, saying that they were seeking the same God as the Jews. The Samaritans were the descendants of the Israelites who before the exile had formed the northern kingdom of Israel. At the time of the destruction of Samaria at the hands of the Assyrians a number of foreigners had come to live there and had inter-married with the Israelites. The resulting race, know as the Samaritans, was, however, mainly Israelite in origin, and retained all the Israelite traditions, including the worship of Yahweh, the ancestral God. In one respect they were different from, and better than, their pre-exilic forefathers, that they had abandoned the idolatrous worship of Yahweh as a golden bull, which in the old days had been practised at Bethel. Unfortunately one bad tradition had been preserved through the centuries, and that was the old jealous feeling that had existed between the northern kingdom of Israel and the southern kingdom of Judah. The southerners showed this spirit of jealousy by pretending that the Samaritans had little or no Israelite blood in them, and that their traditions and religion were heathen—such is the account, written by a southerner, in 2 Kings xvii. The sight of the temple being rebuilt at Jerusalem brought back to the minds of the Samaritans the old days of Solomon when all Israel had worshipped together in one sanctuary. For the moment at any rate their old tribal jealousy was forgotten, and they came, as we have seen, to Jerusalem with the request that they might share in the building of the temple. Now was the opportunity for the Jews to rise above the old tribal jealousy and welcome these people into the religion of Yahweh. Now was the opportunity for Haggai and Zechariah the prophets to claim this request of the Samaritans as the fulfilment of Second Isaiah's words, "They shall fall down before thee, saying, Surely God is with thee." But Haggai and Zechariah were not prophets like the prophets of former days, like Isaiah and Jeremiah, who stood on the right side regardless of king or people. Haggai and Zechariah were made of feebler stuff; they liked to follow rather than lead. Prophecy was in them a dying force: a few equally feeble prophets followed them, and then prophecy ceased altogether. Haggai had the skill of a diplomatist rather than the inspiration of a prophet. He knew that general opinion would be ready to refuse the Samaritan offer; but he needed to have such specious arguments for that course as would satisfy any possible scruples. He began by consulting the priests—

> "If anyone bear holy flesh in the skirt of his garment, and with his skirt touch bread or pottage or wine or oil or any meat, does it become holy?"

and the priests answered, No. Then he asked them—

> "If anyone that is unclean by a dead body touch any of these does it become unclean?"

and they answered, Yes (Haggai ii. 12–13). Anyone who knows the laws of the Old Testament knows that the first answer of the priests was incorrect, for according to Leviticus vi. 27, the flesh of the sin offering made everything it touched holy, and even the water that touched the skirt that touched the holy flesh became holy. Although Leviticus was not published till a later time, it is certain that this law was not an innovation, and the priests could not have been ignorant of it. Why then did they give a false decision? Because they knew what Haggai was really asking—what would happen if unclean Samaritans trod the holy temple courts. Their answer in effect was that the Samaritans would defile the temple if they worked and worshipped there. This conclusion Haggai immediately drew, addressing the whole congregation, and quoting the decision of the priests,

"So is this people, and so is this nation before me, saith Yahweh, and so is every work of their hands, and what they will offer there is unclean" (Hag. ii. 14).

He did not deign to utter the name "Samaritan"; the scornful words, "this people, this nation," perhaps with a wave of his hand northwards, was sufficient indication of the people he was alluding to. The Jews were satisfied. Their tribal jealousy was approved of by the priests and the prophet. But there was one more person to be considered, the Governor Zerubbabel. He would perhaps be unwilling to take an action which might start hostilities between Samaria and Jerusalem, for which he might be called to account by the Persian king. Haggai knew how to persuade him to disregard such fears: he prophesied that the nations were about to be destroyed, and that Zerubbabel would be the Messiah, the Servant of the Lord, and His Chosen One.

"Thus saith Yahweh, I will shake the heavens and the earth; and I will overthrow the throne of kingdoms, and I will destroy the strength of the kingdoms of the nations; and I will overthrow the chariots, and those that ride in them; and the horses and their riders shall come down, every one by the sword of his brother. In that day, saith Yahweh Sabaoth, I will take thee, O Zerubbabel, my servant, the son of Shealtiel, and will make thee as a signet; for I have chosen thee" (Hag. ii. 21-23).

It is possible that the tradition preserved in I Chronicles iii. 17–19, that Zerubbabel was of the royal Davidic line may be true (though his father's name is there given as Pedaiah instead of Shealtiel), and, if true, the fact would give point to the Messianic prediction. Haggai was again supported by

c

Zechariah, who produced a similar prophecy to encourage Zerubbabel, calling him by another Messianic title, "The Branch":

> "Not by might, nor by power, but by my spirit, saith Yahweh Sabaoth. Who art thou, O great mountain? Before Zerubbabel thou shalt become a plain; and he shall bring forth the head stone with shoutings of 'Grace, grace unto it!' The hands of Zerubbabel have laid the foundation of this house; his hands shall also finish it" (Zech. iv. 6–9).

> "Behold the man whose name is the Branch; and he shall grow up out of his place, and he shall build the temple of Yahweh" (Zech. vi. 12).

Any fears that Zerubbabel may have had for the consequences of his action were set at rest by these glowing promises, for we read that an official answer was sent to the Samaritans in the name of Zerubbabel the Governor, Jeshua the High Priest, and the heads of families, to this effect—

> "You have nothing to do with us to build a house unto our God; but we ourselves together will build unto Yahweh, the God of Israel, as king Cyrus, the king of Persia, hath commanded us" (Ezra iv. 3).

It was scarcely to be expected that such an insulting message would be received without enraging the recipients. Some of the Samaritans were so angry that they immediately attempted to stop the work of building by bringing charges against the Jews before Tattenai, the Governor of the whole of Palestine. Fortunately for the Jews, Tattenai did not take the complaint very seriously and allowed the work of building to go on while he made enquiries. He sent a letter to the Persian king, and in due course a reply came enclosing a copy of the

decree of Cyrus permitting the rebuilding of the
temple. Meanwhile the more religious minded
Samaritans, who sincerely wished to join in worship
with the Jews, made several efforts at reconciliation.
The most remarkable of these was an utterance of a
Samaritan prophet which has found its way into
the collection of writings headed "Isaiah" (Isa.
lxiii. 6—lxiv). The most important part of his
speech is as follows:—

"I will make mention of the loving kindness of
Yahweh, and the praises of Yahweh, according to all that
Yahweh hath bestowed on us, and the great goodness
toward the house of Israel, which He hath bestowed on
them according to His mercies, and according to the
multitude of His loving kindnesses. And He said,
Surely they are my people, children that will not deal
falsely. And He became to them a Saviour in all their
affliction. Not an ambassador nor a messenger, but His
presence saved them. In His love and in His pity He
redeemed them" (Isa. lxiii. 7–9).

"Look down from heaven, and behold from the high
dwelling of thy holiness and of thy glory. Where are
thy zeal and thy mighty acts? Restrain not the yearn-
ing of thy bowels and thy tender mercies. For thou
art our Father, for Abraham knoweth us not, and Israel
doth not acknowledge us; thou Yahweh art our Father,
our Redeemer from everlasting is thy name. O Yahweh,
why dost thou make us to err from thy ways, and hard-
enest our hearts from fearing thee? Return for the sake
of thy servants, for the sake of the tribes of thine
inheritance. Why do the wicked march over thy holy
place, and our adversaries trample thy sanctuary? We
have become those over whom thou has not ruled from
all time, those on whom thy name hath not been named.
Oh that thou wouldst rend the heavens and come down
that the mountains might flow down at thy presence!"
(Isa. lxiii. 15—lxiv. 1).

"And we have all become as one that is unclean, and all our righteous acts are as a polluted garment; and we all fade as a leaf; and our iniquities as the wind take us away. And there is none that calleth upon thy name, that stirreth up himself to take hold of thee; for thou has hidden thy face from us, and thou hast delivered us up into the power of our iniquities. But now, O Yahweh, thou art our Father; we are the clay, and thou our potter; and we are all the work of thy hand. Be not wroth very sore, O Yahweh, neither remember iniquity for ever: behold, look, we beseech thee, we are all thy people. Thy holy cities have become a wilderness, Zion hath become a wilderness, Jerusalem a desolation. Our holy and our beautiful house, where our fathers praised thee, is burned with fire, and all our sacred spots are laid waste. Wilt thou refrain thyself for these things, O Yahweh? Wilt thou hold thy peace, and afflict us very sore?" (Isa. lxiv. 6–12).

Readers will notice with interest that the translation given above of lxiii. 9, "Not an ambassador nor a messenger, but His presence saved them," is quite different from that of our ordinary English Bibles. The explanation is that a very slight error has crept into the Hebrew text, spoiling the sense. The correct reading was used by the Greek translators who wrote the Septuagint, and so was translated correctly into the Latin Vulgate, which is reflected in St. Thomas à Kempis' well-known hymn—

> "He sent no angel to our race
> Of higher or of lower place,
> But wore the robe of human frame
> Himself, and to this lost world came."
> *(Ancient and Modern, 173).*

A psalm written at this time in Samaria shows with what earnestness the Samaritans pleaded their cause before God.

"Give ear, O Shepherd of Israel,
   Thou that leadest Joseph like a flock;
   Thou that sittest upon the cherubim shine forth.
   Before Ephraim and Manasseh
   Stir up thy might,
   And come to save us.
   Turn us again, O God of Hosts,
   And cause thy face to shine, that we may be saved"
      (Ps. lxxx. 1–3).

The method of friendly argument with the Jews was
also tried. A deputation from Bethel, presumably
Samaritans,* went to Jerusalem, and pointed out
that ever since the destruction of Jerusalem seventy
years ago they had fasted in commemoration of that
sad overthrow. Surely this was sufficient evidence
of the legitimate interest they had in the temple at
Jerusalem. But they were only met with sarcastic
words from Zechariah, who suggested that their
feasts and fasts were to some other deity than
Yahweh and for their own pleasure (Zech. vii, viii).
For the moment it seemed as if there was no one
among the Jews who would show any sympathy with
the religious longings of the Samaritans. But there
was one man, whose writings are found in Isaiah
lxv.–lxvi. His name we do not know, but he
breathes so much the spirit of Second Isaiah that
we might be inclined to think that Second Isaiah,
whose earlier prophecies had been delivered twenty
years before in Babylon, had now returned to
Judaea and was there making his last great appeal
to his people. He began by addressing the idolaters

---

* The names Sharezer and Regem-melek have been added
from Jer. xxxix. 3 by someone who wished to make it quite clear
that the embassage was heathen.

to whom God was holding out His arms to welcome
them when they turned from their evil ways:

> "I am ready to be enquired of by those who asked not
> for me; I am ready to be found by those who sought me
> not. I said, Here am I, Here am I, unto a nation that
> hath not called on my name. I have spread out my
> hands all the day long unto a rebellious people, who walk
> in a way that is not good, after their own thoughts; a
> people that provoketh me to my face continually,
> sacrificing in gardens, and burning incense upon bricks;
> who sit among the graves, and pass the night in the
> secret places; who eat swine's flesh, and broth of abomin-
> able things is in their vessels; who say, 'Stand by thyself,
> come not near to me lest I sanctify thee.' These are a
> smoke in my nose, a fire that burneth all the day"
> (Isa. lxv. 1–5).

For a moment he turned to the worshippers of
Yahweh, sketching the future of the faithful
remnant:

> "Thus saith Yahweh, As the new wine is found in the
> cluster, and one saith, 'Destroy it not; for a blessing is in
> it,' so will I do for my servants' sakes, that I may not
> destroy them all. And I will bring forth a seed out of
> Jacob, and out of Judah an inheritor of my mountains;
> and my chosen shall inherit it, and my servants shall
> dwell there" (Isa. lxv. 8–9).

Then he turns and proclaims the destruction of the
unrepentant idolaters:

> "But ye that forsake Yahweh, that forget my holy
> mountain, that prepare a table for God, and that fill
> up mingled wine unto Meni; I will destine you to the
> sword, and ye shall all bow down to the slaughter;
> because when I called ye did not answer, when I spake,
> ye did not hear; but ye did that which was evil in mine
> eyes, and chose that wherein I delighted not" (Isa.
> lxv. 11, 12).

"And ye shall leave your name for a curse unto my chosen and the Lord Yahweh shall slay thee, and He shall call His servants by another name: so that he who blesseth himself in the earth shall bless himself in the God of Truth; and he that sweareth in the earth shall swear by the God of Truth, because the former troubles are forgotten, and because they are hid from mine eyes" (Isa. lxv. 15–16).

And then, addressing the true worshippers, he proclaims the glorious and peaceful future of Jerusalem:

"For, behold, I create new heavens and a new earth: and the former things shall not be remembered, nor come into mind. But be ye glad and rejoice for ever over that which I create, for behold, I create Jerusalem a rejoicing and her people a joy. And I will rejoice in Jerusalem, and joy in my people; and the voice of weeping shall be no more heard in her, nor the voice of crying" (Isa. lxv. 17–19).

"The wolf and the lamb shall feed together, and the lion shall eat straw like the ox, and dust shall be the serpent's meat. They shall not hurt nor destroy in all my holy mountain, saith Yahweh" (Isa. lxv. 25).

Having then shown that he will in no wise compromise with heathenism, he turns on the Jewish leaders responsible for building the temple and warns them that the Most High does not dwell in temples made with hands, and that correct ritual apart from a contrite heart is no more acceptable than the ritual of the idolaters:

"Thus saith Yahweh, The heaven is my throne, and the earth the footstool of my feet. Where is the house that ye will build me and where is the sanctuary that shall be my resting place? And all these things, my hand made them, and so all these things came into being, saith Yahweh. But to this one will I look, even to the poor and contrite of spirit, and that trembleth at my word. Killing an ox: slaying a man. Sacrificing a sheep: breaking a dog's neck. Offering an oblation: pouring out swine's blood. Burning frankincense: blessing an idol. Just as they have chosen their ways, and their soul delighteth in their abominations, so will I choose their delusions, and will bring their fears upon them; because when I called, no one answered, when I spake, they did not hear; but they did that which was evil in mine eyes; and chose that wherein I delighted not" (Isa. lxvi. 1–4).

Then he turns to the Samaritans, the faithful ones who are true worshippers, who had been excommunicated by the Jews under the pretence of glorifying Yahweh. The prophet comforts them, and promises rejoicing to those who had mourned over Jerusalem in her adversity.

"Hear the word of Yahweh, ye that tremble at His word: Your brethren that hate you, that cast you out for my name's sake, have said, 'Let Yahweh be glorified that we may see your joy,' but they shall be ashamed. A voice of tumult from the city! A voice from the temple! A voice of Yahweh rendering recompense to his enemies!" (Isa. lxvi. 5–6).

"Rejoice ye with Jerusalem, and be glad for her, all ye that love her. Rejoice for joy with her, all ye that mourn over her; that ye may suck and be satisfied with the breasts of her consolations; that ye may drain out, and be delighted with the abundance of her glory. For thus saith Yahweh, Behold, I will extend peace to her like a river, and the glory of the nations like an overflowing stream. Her children shall be borne upon the side, and shall be dandled upon the knees. As one whom his mother comforteth, so will I comfort you; and ye shall be comforted in Jerusalem. And ye shall see it, and your heart shall rejoice, and your bones shall flourish like the tender grass; and the hand of Yahweh shall be known towards His servants, and He will have indignation against His enemies" (Isa. lxvi. 10–14).

The prophecy concludes with a grand universalistic picture of men of all nations coming to Jerusalem to worship there.

". . . . to gather together all the nations and the tongues; and they shall come, and they shall see my glory. And I will set on them a sign, and those of them who escape I will send unto the nations, to Tarshish, Pul, and Lud, Meshech, and to Tubal, and Javan, to the distant coasts that have not heard my fame nor seen my glory; and they shall declare my glory among the nations. And they shall bring all your brethren out of all the nations for an offering to Yahweh, upon horses, and in chariots, and in litters, and upon mules, and upon swift beasts, unto my holy mountain Jerusalem, saith Yahweh, as the children of Israel bring the offering in a clean vessel unto the house of Yahweh. And of them also will I take for priests and for Levites, saith Yahweh. For as the new heavens and the new earth, which I will make, shall remain before me, saith Yahweh, so shall your seed and your name remain" (Isa. lxvi. 18–22).

As far as we know these great-souled words fell on deaf ears. The temple was finished. The Samaritans were left outside. And Judaism had started on its decline from a spiritual religion to external formalism. In the attempt to keep Yahweh-worship as a religion for themselves alone they robbed it of its power of growth, as if a gardener were to lop off from a tree every green leaf it produced.

NOTES.

On this chapter read Ezra i.; 1 Esdras iv. 47—56, iv. 62—v. 6; Ezra iii. 1—iv. 5, iv. 24—vi. 22; Haggai; Zechariah i.—viii; Isaiah lxiii. 7—lxvi. 22.

Owing to the dislocation of the text of Ezra-Nehemiah and 1 Esdras a few small alterations must be made in reading the text in the order given above. (An explanation of these changes will be found in Torrey's *Ezra Studies*, or in the author's *Early*

Judaism).   In 1 Esdras iv. 47 read, "Then Cyrus the king
wrote letters for him . . ."   In 1 Esdras v. 2, 3 read, "And
Cyrus sent with them a thousand horsemen to bring them to
Jerusalem in safety; and all their brethren, playing upon musical
instruments, drums and cymbals, sent them on their way as
they went up."   In 1 Esdras v. 5, 6 read, "of the priests, the
sons of Phineas and of Aaron, Jeshua son of Josadak, son of
Seraiah; and there rose up with him Zerubbabel, son of Shealtiel,
of the house of David, of the family of Perez, of the tribe of
Judah; in the second year of the reign of Cyrus king of Persia, in
the month Nisan, on the first day of the month."   The original
wording of Ezra iv. 5, 24 was probably, ". . . to frustrate their
purpose all the days of Cyrus king of Persia.   Then ceased the
work of the house of God which is at Jerusalem, and it ceased
until the reign of Darius king of Persia.   Now in the second year
of Darius, Haggai and Zechariah the son of Iddo, the prophets,
prophesied . . ."

Chapter III

HOW THEY BUILT THE CITY WALLS

444 B.C.

WITH the completion of the building of the temple the curtain falls on Jewish history only to be lifted again after some seventy years. Those seventy years were probably as eventful as the seventy years usually ascribed to the exile. As the silence of the exile is broken by the words of Second Isaiah, so the silence that reigns from 520 to 450 B.C. is broken by another unknown writer, to whom we give the name of the Third Isaiah. His writings are to be found in Isaiah xlix. 14–l. 3, and lviii–lxiii. 6. The silence of the exile had been broken by Second Isaiah's call to use the coming deliverance for the glory of God. The silence of this later period was broken by Third Isaiah's call to rebuild the walls of Jerusalem. The contrast is significant: for Second Isaiah, politics were to be consecrated to God; for Third Isaiah, God's favour was to be used for the furtherance of Israel's political aims. Of course the contrast is unfair, for, as we have seen, Second Isaiah stood head and shoulders above his contemporaries; and if we would rightly compare the spirit of 450 B.C. with the spirit of 520 B.C. it would be fairer to compare Third Isaiah with Haggai and Zechariah. Then the contrast is not so marked. At both periods men pinned their faith to stones and mortar. The only difference was that they were

more superstitious about the use of stones and
mortar in 520 B.C.   For at that time they thought
that a well-built temple would ensure the favour of
the Lord, and, as a result, good harvests; while at
the later time they used their stones in the more
practical work of building walls to defend the city
against their enemies.   From a high religious point
of view there is not much to choose between the
two attitudes.   And lest we should be inclined to
think too poorly of the prophets of those days we
must remember that Third Isaiah, like Zechariah,
gave some excellent teaching on social morality.
Yet those who have studied the Old Testament will
know that morality did not grow up in Israel of
itself, but was the fruit of high religion.   The old
prophets, like Isaiah, Micah and Amos, whose moral
teaching thundered over the hills of Judaea and
Samaria, had within them the fire of God.   These
later prophets, like Haggai, Zechariah and Third
Isaiah, repeated the moral teaching of their pre-
decessors, but, lacking the religious fire, could not
produce the thunder.   A psalmist could say in
those days, "There is not one prophet more"
(Ps. lxxiv. 9), and even Third Isaiah himself felt
the lack of real leaders of the people—

> "I looked, and there was none to help, and I wondered
> that there was none to uphold" (Isa. lxiii. 5).

> "He saw that there was no man, and He wondered
> that there was no intercessor" (Isa. lix. 16).

There are some fine passages in Third Isaiah.   One
of the most beautiful is the beginning of chapter lxi.
which our Lord read in the synagogue of Nazareth,

"The spirit of the Lord Yahweh is upon me,
Because Yahweh hath anointed me.
To preach good tidings to the meek He hath sent me,
To bind up the broken hearted,
To proclaim liberty to the captives,
And the opening of the prison to them that are bound;
To proclaim the acceptable year of Yahweh,
And the day of vengeance of our God;
To comfort all that mourn" (Isa. lxi. 1, 2).

The thought is taken from Second Isaiah's poem in xlii. 1–7, and one regrets that there is no mention of Israel being a light to lighten the Gentiles. This of course was a deliberate omission, for in his attitude towards the other nations Third Isaiah rejected the ideals of Second Isaiah. For Third Isaiah the position of the Gentiles must be one of inferiority and of subjection to the Israelites:

"Strangers shall stand and feed your flocks, and aliens shall be your ploughmen and your vine-dressers" (Isa. lxi. 5).

"Strangers shall build up thy walls, and their kings shall minister unto thee" (Isa. lx. 10).

"Kings shall be thy nursing fathers, and their queens thy nursing mothers; they shall bow down to thee with their faces to the earth and lick the dust of thy feet" (Isa. xlix. 23).

In extenuation of this attitude it may be said that Second Isaiah never had to put his ideals into practice as the Israelites were in exile; but that Third Isaiah had to face the practical question of how the stability of the Jewish state would be affected by their attitude towards foreigners. This change in the political condition is well seen in the

geographical outlook. It is true that Second
Isaiah had contemplated the return of Jews from
other places besides Babylonia, but it was to
Babylon that his gaze was chiefly directed. But
Third Isaiah had fixed his gaze on the Great Sea
in the West. From Arabia he expected the Gentiles
to bring their wealth, but no return of Jews was
expected from there, and no mention is made of
Babylon at all. His main interest was in the return
of Jews laden with the fabled wealth of distant
islands.

> "For the abundance of the sea shall be turned unto
> thee; the wealth of the nations shall come unto thee"
> (Isa. lx. 5).

> "Surely the ships shall gather together unto me, with
> the ships of Tarshish in the van, to bring thy sons from
> far, their silver and their gold with them" (Isa. lx. 9).

> "Thou shalt suck the milk of nations and shalt suck
> the breast of kings" (Isa. lx. 16).

> "Ye shall eat the wealth of nations, and in their
> glory ye shall boast yourselves" (Isa. lxi. 6).

The last quotation but one seems almost to be a
deliberate contradiction of the hope expressed in
lxvi. 10–11 in which the friends of Jerusalem are
invited to rejoice in her prosperity,

> "that ye may suck and be satisfied with the breasts of
> her consolations; that ye may drain out and be delighted
> with the abundance of her glory."

It must have been a result of Third Isaiah's
preaching that the first attempt was made to
restore the walls and gates of the city which had not
been standing since the days of Nebuchadnezzar.

Now, there is no use for walls and gates round a city unless it is being attacked by an enemy; so that when a country which is living at peace proceeds to fortify its capital the neighbouring countries immediately want to know what warlike measures are in view. There is always a suspicion that the builders intend aggressive warfare, and are preparing a safe retreat in case of reverse. The building of the walls of Jerusalem at that time was bound to attract immediate attention because the Jews were a subject nation. In the first place they were a part of the Persian Empire, and in the second place they had come to be more or less under the administration of Samaria. The Persian officials at Samaria were the first to be alarmed. They rightly guessed that the primary object of rebuilding Jerusalem was to obtain freedom from Samaritan control, and it was not difficult for them to represent the rebuilding of the city to the Persian king as a threat of rebellion against the imperial power. Ezra iv. 7–23 contains an account of how the Samaritan officials petitioned King Artaxerxes I, and obtained his authority to stop the work.*

From the opening chapter of Nehemiah we learn more about this unsuccessful attempt to rebuild the city walls. For we read that the news was brought to Nehemiah that the walls had been thrown down and the gates burnt. This must have been the forcible way in which the Samaritan officials put an

---

* The student of the book of Ezra should notice that this paragraph about the rebuilding of the city walls in the reign of Artaxerxes I has nothing to do with the rebuilding of the temple in the reign of Cyrus or Darius, and is misplaced in its present position.

end to the work. Nehemiah was filled with great grief when he heard of the failure of the enterprise, and determined to make another attempt himself. Being an extremely astute man, he did not mention the decree forbidding the building of the city, but made his request to the king (in whose service he was) that he might have leave of absence to restore the city in which his ancestors lay buried. A sentimental attachment to his ancestral city, and a desire to see it in a state of good repair, sounded a very different thing from raising a threat of rebellion. The king therefore granted the request, and further, as we learn later, appointed Nehemiah as Governor of Jerusalem. This really was a most important thing, because when Nehemiah was Governor of Jerusalem he was on an equal footing with the Governor of Samaria, both being subject to the Satrap of Syria and Palestine, whose seat was probably at Damascus or Aleppo. It seems that in the period just before Nehemiah's arrival, there had been no Governor of Judaea, and that Sanballat, Governor of Samaria, had exercised the office, and this explains why Sanballat was so angry at Nehemiah's arrival. We have no reason to suppose that any religious question came into the opposition of Nehemiah and Sanballat. The sons of the latter bore names, Shelem-iah and Dela-iah, indicating the worship of Yahweh. The opposition of Sanballat was very natural, and as soon as he learnt Nehemiah's intention of building the walls he accused him of rebellion against the Persian king. But secure in his position, with written authority for the work, Nehemiah had no reason to fear Sanballat, and

sharply ordered him and all his associates to leave
the city, saying, "You have no property, nor
authority, nor proof of citizenship, in Jerusalem."
The story of the rebuilding of the walls is a splendid
example of what can be achieved by one man of
strong determination. When there had been no
such leader the work had been stopped with the
greatest ease. But all Sanballat's strength and
wiles were insufficient when he had to contend with
Nehemiah. Open attacks by soldiers, surprise
attacks in the rear, threats of accusations of treason,
good-natured warnings of threatened assassination,
specious invitations to friendly conference—all in
turn were tried in vain. And in addition to these
external difficulties, Nehemiah had to contend
with the difficulties of insufficient labour, weak
physique of the workers, and (to begin with) the
disappointment of the previous failure. The picture
of men with sword in one hand and builder's trowel
in the other, and of Jewish heads of families taking
their share in the roughest of the work, tells of the
new spirit which Nehemiah the Governor infused
into his people. By the rebuilding of the walls, and
by infusing this patriotic spirit into the Jews, he
not only secured independence from Samaria, but
gained for Judah a new reputation in the eyes of the
other nations. From this time onwards the political
power of Samaria began to wane, and that of Judah
to increase. The judgment of Ben Sira in later days
was well deserved:—

> "Of Nehemiah the memorial is great; who raised up for
> us the walls that were fallen, and set up the gates and bars,
> and raised up our homes again" (Ecclesiasticus xlix. 13).

For us of the present day, who realise that social reform is more important than political change, there is a side of Nehemiah's work which is of greater interest than his freeing Jerusalem from Samaritan political influence.   He undertook a vigorous reform of the social abuses which he found rampant.   The most urgent matter was that lack of patriotic national feeling had led some Jews to take advantage of the poverty of their fellow Jews and enslave some of their children.   Nehemiah had been spending his own money redeeming Jews whom he found working as slaves for foreigners, and now to his disgust he found that it was Jews who had enslaved them in the first case.   When the evil was brought to light, the new sense of brotherhood of the nation was sufficient to check it for the future.   The defence of Jerusalem, now that its walls were built, necessitated a larger number of inhabitants, and Nehemiah persuaded a number of leading men to move into the city, while other families agreed to draw lots for every tenth family to go and live in the city.   One considerable section of the people that used to live in the city was the Levites.   These had been supported out of the tithes which were collected in every village and brought to Jerusalem; but owing to the unsettled state of the government before Nehemiah's arrival the collection of tithes had been neglected, and the Levites had left the city to earn their living on the land.   It must have been a task of some difficulty to reinstitute the custom of tithes, and probably Nehemiah did not undertake it till his second administration.   For after twelve years he went back to Persia, and on his return to

Jerusalem he found that the room in the temple courts intended for collecting tithes had been appropriated by a foreigner Tobiah, with the connivance of the high priest. This discovery led not only to a forcible ejection of the offending Ammonite, but also to the reinstitution of tithing and to an attack on foreign alliances. It is rather strange that both these abuses were also dealt with by the prophet Malachi. He complained that Jews were divorcing their Jewish wives, and it seems probable that they were doing so in favour of foreign wives. Malachi's date is uncertain, but it must have been written near the time of Nehemiah, perhaps shortly before Nehemiah's arrival. The keeping of the sabbath, on which Nehemiah laid great weight, does not happen to be mentioned in Malachi, but it is in line with Malachi's extreme interest in the external side of religion. The question of mixed marriages was not finally settled by Nehemiah, as it had to be taken up again by Ezra. One glaring instance was discovered by Nehemiah, that the grandson of Eliashib the High Priest had actually married the daughter of Sanballat of Samaria. It shows how far we have travelled from the thought of Second Isaiah, that an action which was well calculated to strengthen the religious bonds between the two Yahweh-worshipping communities of Judaea and Samaria was regarded as a most execrable offence against God, and could be spoken of as a defilement of the priesthood and of the Levites (Neh. xiii. 29). Nehemiah was not a priest, but he whole-heartedly took the side of the priests in the age-long struggle between priests and prophets. By this time priesthood was firmly established in Israel as the dominating power, and prophethood was practically extinct. Even Malachi, although included among the books of the prophets, breathes far more the spirit of the priests.

NOTE

On this chapter read Isaiah xlix. 14–l. 3, lviii–lxiii. 6; Nehemiah i.–vii. 5, xi. 1–xiii. 31; Malachi.

Chapter IV

THE TRIUMPH OF THE LAW

NEHEMIAH's first administration lasted from 444 to 432 B.C. His second administration may have been about 430 B.C. As far as our Biblical authorities go, we should have another long gap, some thirty years or so, before the arrival of Ezra. But strange to relate we have in this period two sources of information from outside the Bible, which not only add a few incidents, but give considerable help towards elucidating the vital movements of the period. The first and most important source consists of documents written on papyrus in the Aramaic language, found at Elephantine, an island in the Nile at Assouan, and relating to a Jewish temple that stood on the island. The Jewish colony had had a temple there for at least a century, and probably ever since the days of Jeremiah. This temple was destroyed out of spite by Egyptian priests in 410 B.C., and our documents deal with the attempts of the Jews to get the temple restored. It is always spoken of in the papyri as a temple of Yahweh, but in the temple accounts other deities are mentioned by name; and though most of the Jewish proper names are compounded with "Yahweh," some of them indicate adherence to these other deities. One is reminded of earlier days when Yahweh's uniqueness was not universally recognised; and it seems that in these strange deities, or perhaps

45

consorts of Yahweh, this out of the way place preserved traces of the old polytheism which once had been the popular religion of Israel. They at any rate regarded themselves as orthodox Jews, and in their distress they wrote letters to Bagohi, the Governor of Jerusalem, and to Jehohanan, the High Priest of Jerusalem, and his companions. To these letters they received no reply. It would be interesting to know the reason: was it merely some failure of the postal system? or did the authorities, civil and religious, of Jerusalem hesitate to countenance the practices of Elephantine? It seems that they were not asking for money, nor exactly for authority to build, but for some sort of assurance from recognised Jewish authorities to prove to the Egyptian officials that the worship at Elephantine was the genuine Jewish custom. Failing in their first attempt they wrote again two years later, sending separate letters to the civil authorities of Samaria and Jerusalem. The former letter was addressed to Delaiah and Shelemiah the sons of Sanballat, and the latter to Bagohi. This fact is of the greatest importance to us, because it shows that in the eyes of these colonial Jews the two centres of Jerusalem and Samaria were on an equal footing. The idea never entered their heads that in only one of the two the true religion was practised. More surprising still we find that the two civil authorities, Bagohi and Delaiah, combined in sending a verbal reply, permitting the rebuilding of the temple and the offering of incense and meal-offerings, but implying by their silence that burnt-offerings were not to be allowed. While Nehemiah thought of the Samaritans as heathen, reflecting no doubt the opinion of the priests at Jerusalem, the Governors of the two districts could agree in a common policy as to what was permissible at Elephantine. Nor was the Governor of Judah acting altogether contrary to the Jerusalem priesthood, for there is a letter which was written some years earlier, 419 B.C., giving the Jews of Elephantine instructions for the observance of the passover; and if our reconstruction of a rather tattered papyrus be correct these instructions emanated from the priests of Jerusalem, who must therefore have been more or less in communion with the priests of Elephantine.

The other extraneous source of information is Josephus, who tells a sad story about the high priest Jehohanan. The event must have taken place a few years later, after 404 B.C., as Josephus puts it in the reign of Artaxerxes. Bagoses, doubtless the governor Bagohi whose acquaintance we have made through the Elephantine correspondence, promised to make Jehohanan's brother Jesus high priest in his stead, and when this news reached the ears of Jehohanan he murdered his brother Jesus in the temple. Bagohi naturally inflicted a severe penalty on the Jews for the crime. The incident is interesting as showing how a worldly spirit had entered the priesthood, and that there was a conflict between the civil and the religious heads of the nation. These incidents tell us much of the conditions of Jerusalem, and help us to understand the atmosphere into which Ezra the priest entered when he visited Jerusalem only two or three years later. In our Bibles Ezra appears at the same time as Nehemiah in the reign of Artaxerxes I. It seems that the sources used by the compiler of Ezra and Nehemiah only stated that Ezra came in the reign of Artaxerxes, and the compiler took it to mean the first king of that name instead of the second. People have long felt the historical difficulty in Nehemiah and Ezra being together in Jerusalem. The order of the high priests which were contemporary with these two leaders shows that Ezra belonged to a later generation than Nehemiah, and the date of Johanan the high priest of Ezra's time is confirmed by a contemporary papyrus letter.   See the Chronological Table at the end of the book.

Ezra is an extremely interesting type of man, a type which we come across from time to time in Church History and at the present day.   The general impression people would have of him would be that of a man of strong character based on firm religious convictions.   As a matter of fact, like others of his type, he concealed the weakness of his faith (which was quite genuine as far as it went) by reliance on the material arm.   Quite naively he confesses that he did not really trust God to protect his caravan on the journey to Palestine, and would have liked to have asked for an armed guard, but had not the face to do so after having boasted before the king of the protection of God.   The same character is seen in all his doings in Jerusalem: other men more truly religious might have worked for reform of social abuses by educating public opinion and by inculcating religious ideas; but Ezra had not sufficient belief in the power of religion, or sufficient patience to wait for its slow workings, and preferred to enforce right

conduct by the arm of the law.   He dealt drastically
with the question of foreign marriages that Nehemiah
had concerned himself about.   Unfortunately the
original records of Ezra's work have been much
edited by the compiler of the book of Ezra and
Nehemiah, who was a great admirer of Ezra.   We
cannot help seeing exaggerations in the part said to
have been played by the Persian king in Ezra's
enterprise, and for Ezra's sake we would hope that
the account of the great divorce has been overdrawn.
To the compiler it may have seemed the stern
justice of a brave man to compel all the Jews who
had contracted foreign marriages to send their
wives and children home to their own lands; but to
us it would seem callous bigotry.   But apart from
the details of this action, sufficient is told us about
Ezra to show that he played a part which was to be
of great influence on the future history of the Jews.

The most important and most reliable section of
Ezra's story is told in his own words.   He set out
from Babylonia with a large company of Jews who
had decided to return with him to Palestine.   Ezra's
main purpose was evidently to set in order the
religious life of Jerusalem.   The temple had been
built more than a century before his time, but the
temple feasts were not properly observed, the ancient
laws were not followed, and probably were not
known to the people or taught by the priests.   For
this purpose it was absolutely necessary for Ezra to
have the support of scholars who knew the law books,
and priests who knew how to conduct the sacrifices.
When he gathered the people together, he found to
his horror that none of the clergy had responded to

his call (1 Esdras viii. 42, cf. Ezra viii. 15). He
would not start without any, so he sent back an
urgent message to his brother Iddo asking for
ministers for the temple.   In the old days there was
a tribe or guild called the Levites, all of whom were
qualified to act as sacrificing priests and as teachers
of the law.   But in the early days of the Exile,
the Levites had behaved so badly that Ezekiel
(chapter xliv) said they ought to be degraded to the
position of temple servants, and that none but the
family of Zadok were worthy of offering the sacrifice
at the altar.   This drastic measure was not fully
put into force, for in later times, when the "Priestly
Code" was written, all the descendants of Aaron were
treated as priests, and not only the Zadokites.   In
Ezra's time the matter was not so closely defined,
though there was a distinction between the priests
and the Levites, and there was also a lower class
called the Nethinim, who acted as servants to the
Levites.   Ezra's request to Iddo was successful.
A number of Levites and Nethinim came to join
him; and twelve of the Levites, including Hashabiah
and Sherebiah, were priests (Ezra viii. 24).   Neither
of these two were descendants of Aaron; for by comparing the genealogies given in 1 Chron. vi. it is clear
that they both claimed descent from Levi's third son,
whereas Aaron was supposed to be the grandson of
Levi's second son.   Three-quarters of a century
later, when Neh. xii. was written, recording the list
of high priests up to the time of Alexander the
Great, these two men were entered as Levites and
not as priests.   This fact is of great importance, as
it shows that the Priestly Code was composed after

Ezra's Memoirs were written, and before the time of
Alexander. The only place in the story of Ezra
where the priests are spoken of as sons of Aaron is
Neh. x. 38, which, as can be seen from the tables at
the end of this chapter, is a later addition to the
original account of Ezra's Covenant.

Casiphia, from whence Ezra obtained the ministers
for the temple, is otherwise unknown. One might
guess that it is a Hebrew corruption of Ctesiphon,
the city which later became the capital of the
Parthian Empire. The name is followed by the
Hebrew word *ham-maqom*, "the place," and some
scholars have thought that this is an imitation of a
Babylonian idiom indicating that Casiphia was a
place-name. More probably *maqom* has here its
specialised meaning of "a sanctuary," and if so it
should be translated "the sanctuary in Casiphia."*
We have already seen that the Jews in Egypt had a
temple at Elephantine, where sacrifices were offered;
and if there was such a temple in Babylonia it would
be the very place from which Ezra would seek
priests who not only were students of the law but
also knew the actual practice of the sacrificial cults.

With this addition to the priestly party in Jerusalem, Ezra proceeded to enforce the ritual laws of the
nation. Some time before the Babylonian exile the
ancient stories of the patriarchs had been committed
to writing, not merely for archaeological interest, but
as a framework for the laws, and a certain school of
writers had added a more complete legal code,
particularly in the book of Deuteronomy. This

---

* Cf. Neh. i. 1 "Shushan the palace," i.e. "the palace in
Shushan."

code of laws was still the official code in Ezra's time, though probably more neglected than observed; and Ezra's directions for the observance of the Feast of Booths, and the covenant he drew up for the people, were based entirely on the legislation of Deuteronomy.   But conditions had greatly changed since Deuteronomy was written, and the time had come for a fresh codification of the law.   A clear example is seen in the matter of tithing.   The old law had been that a tithe or tenth of the produce of the fields had been carried by each family to Jerusalem, and there they feasted on it, and the "Levite that was within their gates" shared with them in the feast.   A special provision had been made that if the distance to Jerusalem was too great they might sell the tithe and spend the money on buying fresh provisions for the feast at Jerusalem.   Every third year the tithe was set apart as a kind of poor fund in each village for the benefit of the Levites, strangers, fatherless and widows.   But with the centralisation of the worship at Jerusalem the Levites came to live in Jerusalem, and the custom grew up of bringing the tithe to the temple as an offering to the Levites (including the priests) who lived there.   This is the custom which was supposed to be in force in the days of Nehemiah, Ezra and Malachi; but owing to neglect of tithes many of the Levites had been obliged to leave the city and earn a living in the country.   There was no question now of reviving the ancient custom of making the Levites dependent each on the family with which he lived, and Ezra's reform was directed towards a more efficient collecting of the tithes so that the

Levites could live once more in Jerusalem. How far Ezra altered the method of collecting the tithes we do not know, but three-quarters of a century later, when Chronicles, Ezra and Nehemiah were compiled, the system in vogue was that the Levites accompanied by a priest went round to the villages and collected the tithes and brought them to Jerusalem, and the Levites kept nine-tenths of the tithe for themselves and handed over one-tenth to the priests, who were by that time recognised as a higher rank of the hierarchy. This illustration shows well how change of conditions made changes of the law necessary, and it was some time during the fourth century that these new customs were codified as the "Priestly Code." It used to be thought that Ezra himself was the author of the Priestly Code. Of that we have no evidence, for all his recorded actions are based on the earlier legislation,* but, whether he had any direct hand in it or not, we can be quite sure that it was his influence, probably carried on through his immediate disciples, which brought into being that last stage of Old Testament legislation. It is doubtful whether the Priestly Code ever existed by itself. As we have it now it forms the main structure of the Pentateuch, and all the earlier elements have been built up into it, much as a builder will often utilise for a new building the carved stones of previous buildings. The result is that the Pentateuch, which in its completed form we must regard as the work of the fourth century B.C., reflects the thoughts and ways and laws of many generations of Hebrews, and is in a sense the epitome

* See tables at the end of this Chapter.

of at least five centuries of their cultural history.
The effect of the codification of the Law, and the
completion of the Pentateuch, was probably far
greater than Ezra had imagined when he set the process going.   Jeremiah a long time before had
taught that religion was a thing of the heart, and
had looked forward to the time when men would
know God in their hearts and obey the law that was
written there.   It was an easier thing to ask men
to obey a law written on parchment, and Ezra chose
the easier path, little realising that in so doing he
was weakening the reliance on a personal knowledge
of God.   For us of the present day, who live under
magnificent codes of law by which modern nations
are governed, it may seem at first sight that Ezra
was making a step forward in the direction of
civilization.   But it was not so.   Jewish Law, as
codified in the Pentateuch, is fundamentally different from the laws of modern nations.   Modern laws
are concerned with conduct as between man and
man; they are the terms of agreement by which men
live together in society, and are altered continually
to suit new circumstances and conditions.   Jewish
Law professed to be the full expression of the divine
will, including within its scope, not only the conduct
of man to man, but also the conduct of man to God.
Being regarded as a full statement of God's will for
man the Jewish Law was unalterable; there was no
more room for prophets to come with fresh messages
of God's will, or fresh revelations of His nature;
temporary and permanent legislation were not distinguished; no room was left for individual judgment
in cases not provided for in the Law.   An exact

parallel is seen in the Moslem *shari'a*, the divine law which should (theoretically) bind every Moslem, living in any country, in any century, to the customs which were suited to inhabitants of Iraq and Persia in the eighth and ninth centuries A.D. This Muhammadan law, though supposedly unchangeable, has actually of necessity been changed and largely abrogated in almost every Moslem land.* From this time onwards the Jews looked rather at their sacred scriptures, the Torah or Pentateuch, than at God. To suppose that all God's will could be comprised within the pages of a book was nearly as disastrous as to think that an idol could effectively represent the deity. Religion of the heart, communion with God, became exceedingly difficult. After the conception of holiness as freedom from sin which had appeared in Isaiah vi., it is disappointing to find the Priestly Code descending to the more primitive conception of holiness as a condition which is impaired by physical contact. In Lev. xi. 42–44 the command to be holy is coupled with the prohibition of "unclean" foods such as snakes, lizards and centipedes. This is similar to Haggai's contention that the temple and its worship could be contaminated by the mere presence of Samaritans, and Ezra's belief that the land of Palestine was "unclean," and that mixed marriages of Jews with Gentiles defiled the "holy seed" (Ezra ix. 2, 11). At any time after the final codification of the Law, if a man claimed to speak about God he was met with the question, "Is it in the Book? If so, there is no need

* Full details are given in the author's *The Prospects of Islam*, 1944.

to say it.   If not, it is a lie." The glory of Israel in
the past had lain in its succession of prophets who
were men in touch with the living God.   That spirit
of true religion was not dead, and we shall see as we
continue our story the strange forms in which
religion of the heart was forced to clothe itself now
that the nation had consented to bind itself in the
fetters of the Law.

NOTES.

On this chapter read Ezra vii, viii; Nehemiah vii. 70–viii. 18;
Ezra ix, x; Nehemiah ix, x.

The Feast of Booths. A Table showing that, with the exception
of the last item which is probably an addition by the compiler,
Ezra's regulations for the Feast of Booths followed the Deutero-
nomic legislation (D) rather than that of the Priestly Code (P).:—

Nehemiah viii.	D	P
The date of the Feast 7th mo., 2nd day, Neh. viii. 14.	*of Booths.* JED do not give the date. Pro- bably any time in the 7th mo. Con- trast 8th mo. at Bethel regarded as schismatical, 1 Kings xii. 32, 33.	7th mo., 15th day, Lev. xxiii. 34, Numb. xxix. 12, (also Ezek. xlv. 25).
Blowing of Trumpets No mention.	*and Holy Convocation* No mention	7th mo., 1st day, Lev. xxiii. 24.
Reading of the Law. The Law was read in the 7th mo., from the 1st to the 7th day, Neh. viii. 2, 18.	The Law was to be read at the feast, Deut. xxxi. 11.	No mention.

Nehemiah viii.	D	P
Rejoicing. "Mourn not nor weep" viii. 9. "Neither be ye grieved, for the joy of Yahweh is your strength" viii. 10. "To make great mirth" viii. 12. "And there was very great gladness" viii. 17.	"Thou shalt rejoice in thy feast" Deut. xvi. 14. "And thou shalt be altogether joyful" Deut. xvi. 15.	H has "And ye shall rejoice before Yahweh your God seven days" Lev. xxiii. 40. No mention in P proper.
The Poor. "Send portions unto him for whom nothing is prepared" Neh. viii. 10.	"And the stranger and the fatherless and the widow that are within thy gates" Deut. xvi. 14. "And thy stranger that is within thy gates" Deut. xxxi. 12.	No mention.
Women and children. "Both men and women and all that could hear with understanding," Neh. viii. 2, 3.	"Thou and thy son and thy daughter and thy manservant and maidservant" Deut. xvi. 14. "The men and the women and the little ones" Deut. xxxi. 12.	No mention.
Memorial of the Exodus. No mention.	No mention.	H has "that your generations may know that I made the children of Israel to dwell in booths when I brought them out of the land of Egypt" Lev. xxiii. 43.

Nehemiah viii.	D	P
Day of Atonement. No mention.	No mention.	7th mo., 10th day, the great Day of Atonement, Lev. xxiii.27-32, Numb. xxix. 7–11.
The Eighth Day. "And on the eighth day was a solemn assembly according unto the ordinance" Neh. viii. 18. This is probably an addition by the Chronicler, who made the same addition in another place, changing "On the 8th day he sent the people away" 1 Kings viii. 66 into "On the 8th day they held a solemn assembly" 2 Chron. vii. 9.	No mention.	"On the 8th day shall be a holy convocation unto you" Lev. xxiii. 36. "On the 8th day ye shall have a solemn assembly Numb. xxix. 35.

Ezra's Covenant. A Table showing that the original form of Ezra's Covenant was based on Deuteronomy and the earlier legislation, and that the items corresponding to the Priestly Code are later additions to the original Covenant:—

Neh. x.	JED	P
x. 30 Not to intermarry with foreigners.	D, Deut. vii. 3.	No mention.
x. 31 Not to trade on the sabbath.	Work on the sabbath was forbidden in all the codes.	
x. 31 To forgo the 7th year.	E, Ex. xxiii. 11. D, Deut. xv. 1–11.	Lev. xxv. 1–7.
x. 31 To forgo all debts in the 7th year.	D, Deut. xv. 2.	No mention.
x. 32 To pay one-third of a shekel temple tax.	Not in JED.	Not in P. P has one-half shekel temple tax. Ex. xxx. 13, xxxviii. 26.
[x. 33. An addition giving the purposes of the temple tax: shew-bread, continual meal offering, continual burnt offering, holy things, sin offerings.]	Not in JED.	Shewbread, Lev. xxiv. 5f. Continual meal and burnt offerings, Ex. xxix. 38–42. Sin offerings, Lev. vii. 37.
x. 34 To bring in wood offering by lot.	No mention in the Pentateuch.	
x. 35–36 To bring first-fruits of ground and of fruit trees, of sons and of cattle, of herds and flocks.	First fruit of ground. E, Ex. xxiii. 19, D, Deut. xxvi. 2, 10. Sons and cattle, E, Ex. xxii, 29-30. Herds and flocks, D, Deut, xii. 6.	Sons and cattle, Ex. xiii. 2.

Neh. x.	JED	P
[x. 37–39a betrayed as an addition by starting the list again after it had been rounded off with the words "to bring to the house of our God, unto the priests that minister in the house of our God," and by repeating the first fruit of the fruit of trees which had been already mentioned. x. 37 Tithes of coarse meal and heave offerings.]	No mention.	Numb. xv. 20 (also Ezek. xliv. 30).
x. 39b Not to forsake the house of God.	Many references in D and P.	

Chapter V

THE INVASION OF GREEK THOUGHT

THE fourth century B.C. saw the disintegration of
the Persian Empire, and Palestine must have been
constantly disturbed by the march of armies. The
comparative seclusion of the Jews in their mountain
home accounts for the fact that during those
troublous years it was possible to find leisure for
the completion of the Torah; and it is scarcely surprising that opportunity was not found for writing
the history of their own times. Very probably a
number of the psalms were produced in those days,
but it is a difficult thing to ascertain the date of
psalms. About the middle of the century there was a
general revolt of subject races against the Persian
king, and the proud city of Sidon suffered a most
dreadful fate, the inhabitants burning their houses
over their heads rather than fall into the hands of
Artaxerxes Ochus. We are not told whether Judaea
was implicated in the revolt, but Greek historians
have preserved for us the fact that at that time
Ochus transplanted some of the Jews to the neigh-
bourhood of the Caspian Sea. Only a few years
later the Persian Empire fell before the arms of the
conquering host of Alexander the Great, and again
the sea-coast towns suffered terribly: Tyre was sacked
after a seven months' siege, and its inhabitants slain
or sold into slavery. During the siege Alexander demanded assistance from Jaddua, the high priest at
Jerusalem, which he refused on the grounds of his

oath of allegiance to the Persian king. Such a refusal
would naturally have led to severe punishment, but
somehow the Jews managed to get reconciled to the
conqueror—according to the account of Josephus,
Alexander was impressed by the sight of the high
priest and the priests coming out in procession in
their robes to meet him—and the calamity was
averted. The Samaritans readily offered their help
to Alexander, and in return were granted permission
to build a temple on Mount Gerizim. From this
event must be dated the definite schism between the
Samaritans and the Jews. The Pentateuch, as we
have seen, was already completed, and so the
Samaritans had already accepted it before the
schism took place. The remaining books of the Old
Testament were not regarded as sacred scripture till
a later date, and have never been accepted by the
Samaritans.

Up till this time the wars of the nations round
about Palestine left Judaea as a rule more or less
untouched. Armies marched along the high road
through Philistine country, and waged battles in the
Plain of Megiddo, but did not generally turn aside
to meddle with the peculiar people who lived in
Jerusalem and its neighbouring hills. Even the
sack of Jerusalem by Nebuchadnezzar had not inter-
fered with the life of the Jews as much as we used
to think.

Stranger still, the two centuries 538 to 333 B.C.,
during which Judaea was part of the Persian Empire,
left but little impress of Persian religion or culture.
This fact is less surprising when we learn that the
Greek historian Herodotus, who visited Persia in the

time of Nehemiah, wrote an account of Persian religion which has no resemblance to Zoroastrianism, but is evidently the Indo-Iranian polytheism which Zoroaster had tried to reform some four or five centuries earlier. It seems probable that Zoroaster's pure monotheism found few followers, and those only in Eastern Persia, until the priesthood known as the Magi adopted the religion, or as much of it as they could reconcile with their more primitive ideas, and popularised it. It then spread Westwards, and from the time of Darius I was adopted as the court religion. Though never idolatrous, this Magian religion had features, including magic and astrology, which would not have commended it to the Jews, whereas, had they known Zoroaster himself, they could scarcely have refrained from numbering him amongst the true prophets of God. As it was, the most that Persia contributed to Judaism was the doctrine of angels, and possibly some development of the Messianic hope.

It was otherwise with the great Greek invasion. No part of Western Asia could remain unaffected by the conquests of Alexander. Hitherto one oriental despot had succeeded to another; but the new invasion was the impact of a different civilization, a civilization that was rooted in philosophy, and was founded on city life. It may only be compared with the invasion of Arab forces nine hundred years later. Those Arab forces were bound together by religion, and that binding force brought a unity of government to almost the same area that became subject to Alexander. Alexander's followers had nothing like the religion of Islam to act as a unifying and binding force, so that after his early death there was nothing to hold together under one government the vast tract of country from the Indus to the Mediterranean Sea, which had fallen to his arms. But though lacking the force of religion, the Greek invasion had brought a new outlook on life, a new energy, which changed the face of Western Asia. The influence on Judaism was not apparent at first; but the seeds were sown which three centuries later enabled Christianity to burst the bonds of a national cult, and to appear as a world-religion which was the inheritor of the deepest religious experience of Asia and of Europe. Alexander's death was the signal for a struggle for power between his generals. Politically speaking the next half century was chaotic, ending in the establishment of the Ptolemies as the rulers of Egypt and the Seleucids as the rulers of all the lands from Syria to Afghanistan. Between the two lay Palestine, important for both as a highway and a bulwark. Sometimes one, sometimes the other, would be the suzerain to whom the Jews had to pay tribute. But whether for the time the Jews recognised a Ptolemy in Egypt or a Seleucus or an Antiochus in Antioch as their ruler, the cultural effect was the same. For both were Greek kingdoms, breathing the spirit of the philosophic West. Much though we may regret the absence of Jewish history during the third century B.C., we may comfort ourselves with the thought that no contemporary historian could have described the infiltration of Greek ideas, and the interplay of these with the ancient religion of Israel, which was the really important event of the time. Daniel xi. 3–4, written a long time afterwards, describes briefly the rise and fall of Alexander:—

> "And a mighty king shall stand up, that shall rule with great dominion, and do according to his will. And when he shall stand up, his kingdom shall be broken, and shall be divided towards the four winds of heaven; but not to his posterity, nor according to his dominion wherewith he ruled; for his kingdom shall be plucked up, even for others besides these."

The verses that follow tell of the tramp of armies through the land, the armies of the Seleucids in the north and the Ptolemies in the south, wars that harassed but did not otherwise affect the children of Israel. The varying fortunes were finally settled in 223 B.C. when Antiochus III (the Great), having taken Gaza after a long siege, became master of Palestine. This event is referred to in Daniel xi. 16:

> "He that cometh against him shall do according to his own will, and none shall stand before him: and he shall stand in the glorious land, and in his hand shall be destruction."

Somewhere about that time there was a high priest named Simon the son of Onias (or Johanan), whose praises are sung in Ecclesiasticus l. Compared with some of the worthless money-grubbing leaders who, if we are to believe Josephus, were characteristic of the period with which we have been dealing, Simon's simple honesty, his care for the security of the city, and his venerable appearance, were remembered afterwards as the type of the ideal high priest and ruler:—

> "Great among his brethren, and the glory of his people,
> Was Simeon, the son of Johanan, the priest,
> In whose time the house was renovated,

And in whose days the temple was fortified;
In whose time a reservoir was dug,
A water cistern like the sea in abundance.
In his days the wall was built,
With turrets for strength like a king's palace.
He took thought for his people (protecting them) from
    spoliation,
And fortified his city against the enemy.
How glorious was he when he looked forth from the Tent
And when he came out of the sanctuary.

.   .   .

Then he came down and lifted up his hands
Upon all the congregation of Israel,
And the blessing of Yahweh was upon his lips,
And in the name of Yahweh he glorified himself.
And a second time they fell down, (now) to receive
The pardon of God from him."

It was either this man or his grandfather who is
mentioned in Pirke Aboth i. 2, according to which
he used to say, "On three things the world standeth,
on the Torah, and on the Service, and on the doing
of kindnesses." He is thus represented as equally
balancing the legal side of religion (the Torah), the
ritual side (the Service), and the prophetical side
(duty to one's neighbour), and this would well fit a
time before the rise of the sects of the Pharisees and
Sadducees. Another Simon, a man of a very
different stamp, is represented to us as the villain of
the piece in the story of Heliodorus in 2 Maccabees iii.
The Second Book of Maccabees is a fairly late work,
whose author delights in the marvellous and has little
regard for the difference between fact and fiction.
Undoubtedly some facts underlie his story, and it
may well be true that Simon for his own ends told
tales in the Seleucid court of the fabulous wealth

of the temple, and that Heliodorus was sent to gather the plunder and was frustrated of his purpose. The heavenly apparition in golden armour who gave the plunderer a good thrashing, and the intercession of the high priest to God that Heliodorus's life might be spared, may be dismissed as the inventions of a writer who wished that evil-doers always got their deserts. The same Heliodorus later murdered the king, whose prime minister he was, but was not strong enough to seize the throne for himself, for Antiochus IV, a brother of the murdered king, returned from abroad and took the kingdom about 175 B.C. Of this Antiochus we shall have much to say in the next chapter.

Although the list of historical events in Jewish history for the two centuries ending 175 B.C. is so meagre, the period was probably as important as any other two centuries for the development of Judaism. The beginning of the period saw, as we have said, the completion of the Pentateuch. Before the end of the period the second large collection of Old Testament scriptures, known as the Prophets (i.e. Joshua, Judges, Samuel, Kings, and the prophetical books proper), was gathered together and reckoned as Scripture; and at least a large part of the Writings (the remaining books of the Old Testament) had been composed. Of the Writings two parts are worthy of special mention. The Psalms were religious songs or hymns which had been written from time to time and were gathered into collections mainly for use in the temple. Many of these must have had their origin in the period under discussion, though some were earlier, and probably a few were later. They stand as a monument of Israel's religion in a way that no other part of the Old Testament does, for they were the actual lifting-up of the Hebrew soul in worship; and it is well to remember that, while politics were in turmoil, and deep problems of life and doctrine were being thrashed out, the heart of the people was all along set on its God. The other part of the Writings to which we must allude is the Wisdom Literature. As soon as the Jews came in contact with Greeks they must have heard of the place that wisdom occupied in Greek thought. We need not suppose that they took the trouble to read Greek philosophy; but the praise of wisdom led them to think once more of their ancestral faith and to look at it from a new point of view as the highest expression of wisdom. "The fear of the Lord is wisdom," epitomised the result of their thought. That sentence alone shows how far the Wisdom writers were away from Greek thought, for Greek wisdom was the highest achievement of the intellect, but the Hebrews regarded wisdom as that spur to right conduct which comes from reverent submission to God. The term "fear of God" is one that has its roots in ancient times when men were literally afraid as they stepped over the threshold of the sanctuary of God; and as the conception of God deepened, the idea of the fear of God deepened into the sense of true religion, but religion coupled with awe of a personal God. To keep the commandments of the Law would be a natural consequence of fearing God, but the fear of God was a much greater thing than obedience to a code of laws. When we read the rather prosy good advice of Ecclesiasticus or

Proverbs, and are inclined to think it commonplace, it is worth while to stop and consider that here is something that goes deeper than mere obedience to the Law. The hundred and nineteenth Psalm with its 176 verses in praise of the law, the statutes and the judgments, may refer to the written code of laws, or to God's revelation in a fuller sense; but when Ben Sira in the book of Ecclesiasticus teaches his hearers to observe good manners at the dinner table and to honour the physician, we feel certain that he is bringing religion into everyday life and is not content with keeping the written commandments. The Book of Job, on the face of it a philosophic treatise on the origin of suffering, in reality is based on the same conception of the fear of God; for having denied the current theory that suffering is the direct consequence of one's own sins as contrary to experience, and having refused to believe in an unjust God as contrary to true religion, and having no solution in reward and punishment after death, it finds satisfaction in the sense of reverential awe that the creature must have before his Creator. It is interesting to find that in the Bhagavadgita, the most deeply loved monument of Indian religious thought, Arjuna, the hero of the poem, finds his satisfaction amidst the conflicting claims of philosophy and mysticism, in a similar vision of God in all His numinous and awful majesty. In a similar way, though not as impressively as Job or the Bhagavadgita, that strange book Ecclesiastes, which can see no purpose or plan in life, which breathes a spirit of agnosticism, denying (ix. 2) the reward of the righteous or the punishment of the wicked, comes back to the sense of awe in the presence of God:—

> "Remember also thy Creator in the days of thy youth,
> Ere the evil days come,
> And the years draw nigh, when thou shalt say,
> I have no pleasure in them" (Eccles. xii. 1).

> "The end of the matter: all hath been heard:
> Fear God and keep His commandments:
> For this is the part of every man" (Eccles. xii. 13).

The problem that the Wisdom writers grappled with was incapable of solution without a belief in the future life, and we must remember that right up to the end of the period dealt with in this chapter the Jews had no doctrine of resurrection. Beyond death there was only the darkness of Sheol, that fancy of primitive man who gets his notions of what there is after death by analogy with the cold dark earth in which the corpse is laid. Ben Sira, in common with most of the people of his day, believed that there would be complete retribution in this life for our good and evil deeds:—

> "Delight not in the delights of the ungodly;
> Remember that they shall not go unpunished to Sheol"
>   (Ecclesiasticus ix. 12).

Job equally strongly denies this doctrine. But neither Job nor Ben Sira thought of recompense in another world. For Ben Sira the reward of a good man whom the world has not recognised lies with his descendants:—

> "Nevertheless these were men of piety,
> And their hope hath not ceased;
> With their seed their goodness remaineth sure,
> And their inheritance to their children's children"
>   (Ecclesiasticus xliv. 10–11).

From time to time Christians have held out the hope of heaven or the fear of hell as the main motive for good conduct. It is worth while to remember that the magnificent morality of the Old Testament was altogether independent of any such hopes or fears, and rested solely on the desire to do the will of God. One of the high priests in those days is reported to have said,

> "Be not like slaves who serve the master with a view to receiving a present; but be like slaves who serve the master not with a view to receiving a present; and let the fear of heaven be upon you" (Pirke Aboth i. 3).

For him, as for the Wisdom writers, the fear of heaven, or, as we should say, reverent submission to God, was sufficient motive for right conduct.

NOTE.

On this chapter read Daniel xi.; Ecclesiasticus 1; 2 Maccabees iii.

Chapter VI

MARTYRS FOR THE FAITH

168 B.C.

No one reading Ecclesiasticus would think that the invasion of Greek thought was a menace to Judaism. So quietly had the foreign influence crept in that the godly Jews scarcely thought of it as a force to be reckoned with. Ben Sira realised that many people were neglecting the true religion, but he does not seem to have realised that Hellenism was a positive force, something like the force of a religion, which was drawing men to it and was setting itself up as a substitute for the divine law. He was a representative of a party, who presently were to come into prominence under the name of the Hasidim or Godly. The last two centuries had seen the development of the synagogue, where the Law of God was read and studied. In the earliest days of Israel's occupation of Canaan, religion filled a place in the life of every village, but it was a religion that had its centre in the high places, with their idolatry and often licentious rites; and the reformers of the eighth and seventh centuries had made a clean sweep of it all by destroying the high places and concentrating all the worship at Jerusalem. By the rise of the synagogue religion had once more come to the villages, but a religion of high and stern morality. The result of this was that in the second century B.C. the real strength of the nation's religion did not rest with the priests who directed the sacrificial cultus of the capital, but with the country folk who studied the Law in their synagogues. Occasionally of course men in high position were found on the side of these Hasidim, and when Antiochus Epiphanes ascended the Seleucid throne there was such a man as high priest. His name was Onias, and he is said to have been the son of the high priest Simon, whom we have already mentioned. He was in the succession of those who from old times had handed on the lamp of truth. At the beginning of the Jewish work known as Pirke Aboth we read—

> "Moses received the Torah from Sinai and delivered it to Joshua, and Joshua to the elders, and the elders to the prophets, and the prophets delivered it to the men of the Great Synagogue. They said three things, 'Be deliberate in judgment; raise up many disciples; and make a fence for the Torah.' Simon the Just was one of the remnants of the Great Synagogue."

As far as we know there never was actually a body known as the Great Synagogue, but the tradition probably reflects faithfully the opinions of the leaders in the fourth and third centuries. They founded schools where the Law was studied with careful deliberation, and where its provisions were amplified to suit every possible circumstance that might arise.

It was the ambition of Antiochus Epiphanes to weld together his kingdom on the basis of Greek culture, a culture, as we have said, that belonged chiefly to city life. While the Hasidim had been quietly developing their devotion to the Law, the young men of Jerusalem were adopting the new

fashions, developing their bodies after the Greek
manner in the gymnasium, playing Greek games,
wearing Greek clothes, and no doubt despising the
religion of their fathers as an out-of-date superstition.
Antiochus thought to encourage this process of
Hellenization, and did not realise the strength of the
old religion hidden away in the villages and among
the poor. It was easy to depose the high priest
Onias, and put in his place his brother Jason, who
was a leader in the Hellenizing movement. Greek
games in themselves were not immoral, nor contrary
to true religion (though Greek culture in the East
was rather apt to appear at times in a debased
and sometimes even vicious form) and we need not
think of Jason as deliberately working against the
Jewish faith. Indeed there is a suggestion that
he had too many religious scruples to carry out
Antiochus's policy, for presently we find Jason
deposed and a thoroughly unscrupulous man
named Menelaus in his place. A little later Jason
made the foolish mistake of raising a revolt against
Menelaus and against the Seleucid powers, hoping
to rely on Egypt. This folly brought Antiochus to
Jerusalem in wrath. He plundered the temple,
and made the fateful decision to hasten by force the
"civilizing" process, as he would have called it, of
the Jews. There is no doubt that the influence of
Hellenism had been growing stronger in the city;
and one can only speculate how much further it
would have gone before a reaction set in against it.
But the hasty action of Antiochus showed in clear
colours the true nature of this boasted civilization.
The Jews, who just before had thought of it as

mainly a question of dress and athletic training, now
saw that it meant the substitution of Olympian
Zeus for Yahweh as the object of worship.   In the
eyes of every Jew it was "the abomination of
desolation" when a sow was sacrificed on an altar
built on the top of the altar of burnt offering (Dan.
xi. 31).   With unexpected suddenness the fire of
persecution swept over the land: circumcision was
prohibited, the books of the Law were destroyed, and
the attempt was made to exterminate everything
that the Jew, whether from the national or from the
religious point of view, held dear.   The Jews read in
their scriptures how their ancestors had been enslaved in Egypt; how heathen rites had been intro-
duced by Manasseh; they had dim memories of how
their fathers had been torn from their homeland and
transplanted to Babylon.   But never before had they
known the necessity of choosing between a denial of
their faith and a martyr's death.   Little did Antiochus dream of the strength in character and numbers
of those who fled from the persecution and, when
brought to bay, preferred death to apostasy.
Neither he nor anyone else could have foreseen the
strange alliance by which the pious Hasidim sub-
mitted to the leadership of the Maccabean patriots
and fought with them the battle for freedom.

The story is told in 1 Maccabees iii., how the aged
Mattathias refused to join in the idol worship, and
slew the officer who had come to enforce it; and
how he and his sons fled to the mountains where
they were joined by all who resisted the oppression.
Of these a large proportion were Hasidim, and we
have a touching scene of their refusing even to

defend themselves on the sabbath day and dying
without resistance. Not out of love for their
enemies, but out of reverence for the Law, they
turned their cheeks to the smiter; and if the motive
was less noble than the love for our fellows, which
our Saviour taught us, we cannot withhold our
admiration and amazement. However, Mattathias
and his sons persuaded them that they would not
attain their end by that means, and after that they
consented to fight even on the sabbath day. The
old man Mattathias did not long survive, and his
son Judas the Maccabee became the leader. Fighting first against the forces of the enemy which were
already in the land, he won several victories. The
authorities in Antioch perceived the seriousness of
the situation, and a general named Lysias was sent
with a large army to attack Judas. In two succes-
sive years Lysias was defeated, or at any rate on the
second occasion retired to Antioch without having
suppressed the rebels. His return was probably
hastened by the news of the death of Antiochus
Epiphanes. After his departure the Jews were free
to practise their religion again, and on the 25th day
of the month Chislev in 165 B.C., the third anniver-
sary of the desecration, the altar was restored and
re-dedicated. The festival of the Dedication, or
the Feast of Lights, has been observed ever since
in commemoration of the great deliverance (see
St. John x, 22). Immediately after this, Judas
organised raids into the other parts of Palestine
with the double purpose of gathering together such
Jews as would join his cause, and gaining wealth by
plundering the other inhabitants. The question

immediately comes to our minds, Who were these
Israelites whom Judas found in Galilee and the other
side of Jordan?   We have learnt in recent years
that the Samaritans were mostly of the old Israelite
stock; and it is quite likely that when the Assyrian
deportations took place there were numerous
Israelites left in other parts of the Northern Kingdom
as well as Samaria.   The policy of Judas now was
to gather together such of the Israelites as were
willing to stand up for their national religion against
the oppressor.   Others no doubt there were with
some Israelite blood in them who had no care for
the old faith, but these naturally would not follow
Judas.   There is no mention of his bringing in any
Israelites from Samaria, for though they were
worshippers of the same God, and acknowledged the
same Law, the ancient enmity could not be forgotten.
Ben Sira a few years earlier reckoned the Samaritans,
along with the hereditary enemies of Philistia and
Edom, as the most contemptible of men:—

"Against two nations doth my soul feel abhorrence,
 And against a third which is not a people:
 The inhabitants of Seir and Philistia,
 And that foolish nation which dwelleth in Sichem"
     (Ecclesiasticus l. 25–26).

According to 1 Maccabees, Judas committed great
massacres during these operations; and the Hasidim
must have begun seriously to consider whether
they were justified in following such a leader.
Moreover Judas was still opposed by a Hellenising
party of the Jews who held the citadel of Jerusalem
against him.   The Syrian general Lysias came down
in force, and the defeat of Judas seemed certain.

But Lysias was obliged to return to Antioch to defend his position there, and before leaving made a covenant with the Jews granting them religious liberty in exchange for political submission. These terms were very acceptable to the Hasidim who had no mind to support Judas for purely political ends.

These few years in which the religion of the Jews was put to the test, and the strength of quiet devotion was proved, not only demonstrated to the world that Judaism contained something which was not to be found in other faiths, but also added the coping stone to Judaism. For in the midst of the terrors of those days the revelation of life beyond the grave suddenly shone out; and, once declared, it so obviously supplied what was lacking in Judaism that it was accepted by the majority of the nation as soon as it was whispered, and became the most prominent doctrine in the literature of the succeeding centuries. The book of Daniel was written at the time of crisis, between the desecration of the temple and its restoration, to encourage the righteous to maintain the faith in the face of persecution. In one image after another the author depicted the righteous resisting the impious commands of persecutors, bearing suffering at their hands, and finally coming out victorious. The stories of Daniel, of Shadrach, Meshach and Abednego are not what we should call history: they are rather imaginative pictures calculated to rouse the faithful to hold bravely to their faith in God against the attacks of the heathen. The crisis demanded something more than the Wisdom Literature. It was so obviously untrue that the righteous always have the best of this life, and that the wicked are in the end cut down in the prime of life like the felling of a green bay tree. Some fresh motive was needed to make men adhere to the Law of God, something more than wise moral counsels. And the new motive was the knowledge that for those who forsook the Law there was laid up in store shame and everlasting contempt, and for the godly an awakening to everlasting life (Dan. xii. 2).

The compact made by Lysias with the Jews did not last long, for a certain Demetrius, of the royal Seleucid house, who had been a hostage at Rome, returned and seized the reins of government from Lysias. The change of government encouraged the Hellenistic party of the Jews, who looked with disfavour on Judas; and they put forward one of their number named Alcimus and persuaded Demetrius to make him high priest. Now the Hasidim, whose allegiance to Judas had been weakening, felt that it would be safe to have Alcimus as high priest, because, though a Hellenist, he was of the old high-priestly family. It is strange that by now they had not learnt that Hellenism and the Jewish faith were ill-mated companions. They soon had cause to repent their acquiescence in Alcimus's appointment, for he used his power unmercifully and shed much blood. Still they would not have joined Judas again, but for one of those blundering errors that foreign rulers are sometimes capable of. For Nicanor, the general whom Demetrius sent to capture Judas, threatened to turn the temple into a temple of Dionysus if the Jews did not hand over Judas. This of course was an unreasonable request, for the priests were not in a position to lay hands on Judas;

and the threat to the temple brought all the Hasidim
back again on to Judas's side. A great battle was
fought, in which the Hasidim showed the bravery of
religious frenzy,

> "for their fear for wives and children, and furthermore
> for brethren and kinsfolk, was in less account with them;
> but greatest and first was their fear for the consecrated
> sanctuary" (2 Macc. xv. 18).

Nicanor was slain in the battle, and the day of
Judas's greatest victory was celebrated for many
years as "Nicanor's Day." Directly after the
battle, Judas decided on a new step, and sent an
embassage to Rome to make an alliance against the
Seleucid kings. It was the old policy which the Jews
in the days of the kingdom had so often tried of
dabbling in foreign politics, running off to seek help
from Egypt or from Babylonia, a policy which the
prophets had always spoken against. In this case,
as in the olden days, the alliance did no good, for
before Rome could come to the rescue Demetrius
had sent an overwhelming force to punish Judas.
By this time Judas had lost most of the support of
the Jews. He was left with a much diminished
army, was defeated, and slain in battle. At the
moment the death of Judas seemed to the Jews a
catastrophe, and the laudatory epitaph of the
historian of the Maccabees may only slightly
exaggerate the feelings of the time:—

> "And they bewailed him, and all Israel made great
> lamentation for him, and mourned many days and said,
> How is the mighty fallen, the saviour of Israel! And the
> rest of the acts of Judas and his wars, and the valiant

deeds which he did, and his greatness, they are not written; for they were exceeding many" (1 Macc. ix. 20–22).

But the kingdom of heaven is not won with the sword, and Judas is scarcely remembered in later Jewish records.

NOTE.

On this chapter read 1 Maccabees i–ix. 22; 2 Maccabees iv–xv.

Chapter VII

EXTENDING THE BORDERS OF ISRAEL

THE Seleucid Empire had shrunk to small dimensions, compared with what it was at its commencement; and in the period on which we enter after the death of Judas the internal dissensions of the Seleucids gave opportunity for the exercise of skilful diplomacy on the part of the Jewish leaders. In former times when Ptolemies and Seleucids had struggled for possession of Judaea, it had been treated as a chattel to be fought or bartered for. But with the decay and division of the Seleucid power, Judaea entered the arena of politics, playing the game of diplomacy herself, and offering herself as an ally now to one side, now to the other. Jonathan the brother of Judas the Maccabee, was the leader in these intrigues. We need not concern ourselves with the details. Jonathan professed allegiance to four rulers in turn, changing sides three times, and each time exacting some fresh privilege from the ruler whom for the moment he favoured. From the first, Demetrius I, he received recognition as a lawful leader of armed forces; from the second, Alexander Balas, he secured appointment as the Jewish high priest; from the third, Demetrius II, he got remission of tribute in exchange for a large cash payment, and a piece of Samaritan territory was transferred to Judaea; from the fourth he got recognition as a general in the king's army, and got his brother

Simon appointed Governor of Palestine. This last ruler, whose name was Tryphon, discovered Jonathan's duplicity, and arrested him, and afterwards executed him. But Simon's position as Governor of Palestine was so secure that he was able to lead the Jews to still greater triumphs, improving the defences of Jerusalem, and extending the boundaries of his rule. In particular it may be noted that he ejected the Gentile inhabitants of Joppa and made it a purely Jewish town. Simon followed the turncoat policy of his brother, and got from Demetrius II even more complete immunity from tribute than had been granted by the same king to Jonathan. The final triumph was marked by the surrender of the Seleucid garrison, which up till that time had held out in the citadel of Jerusalem. It seemed as if this was the end of Seleucid domination, and the Jews rejoiced exceedingly. Hitherto, Simon, like his brother Jonathan, had only been high priest by the will of the foreign rulers. But now the priests and people solemnly appointed him as high priest for ever "until there should arise a faithful prophet" (1 Macc. xiv. 41), and they thought that a new and glorious era dawned. A temporary set-back resulted from the rise of a stronger king, Antiochus Sidetes, in place of Demetrius. He claimed damages from the Jews for their capture of Joppa and of Gazara or Gezer (whose inhabitants had been ejected like those of Joppa). Simon refused the full amount, and for the moment it seemed as if the king would not be able to enforce his demands. But presently a large army attacked Jerusalem and the city surrendered. By that time

John Hyrcanus had succeeded his father as high priest, Simon having been assassinated by an ambitious son-in-law. Sidetes treated the Jews very leniently, and we may conjecture that pressure had been brought to bear on him by Rome, as we know that the Jewish leaders had been sending embassies to Rome repeatedly. For four or five years, Sidetes was nominally master of Palestine, but after his death such disorder reigned at Antioch, that the Jews enjoyed complete freedom which lasted from 129 B.C. till the conquest of Jerusalem by Pompey in 63 B.C.

John Hyrcanus, though still continuing to call himself high priest, was chiefly a warrior and man of blood. He extended the borders of Judaea on all sides, attacked the Samaritans who dwelt in Shechem and destroyed their temple on Mount Gerizim. An attack on the Gentiles who lived in the city of Samaria brought on fresh complications with Antioch, in spite of which his sons, who were in charge of the operations, were able to raze the city to the ground. An operation of greater interest to us is the forcible conversion of the people of Idumaea to Judaism. We know so little of the history of Idumaea that it is impossible to say whether these people were of old Edomite stock, or whether there was any admixture of Israelite blood. Hyrcanus's son Aristobulus, who succeeded him (the first to take the title of king), pursued the same policy with the Ituraeans in Galilee of the Gentiles, where perhaps we should rather expect to find some remains of the old Israelite stock. It will of course be realised that neither Hyrcanus nor his son had any missionary motive. Their only thought was to extend the borders of their kingdom. They were only putting into action what pious Jews had hoped for for many a long year. The following verses by Ben Sira date from a century earlier, and yet they might almost be a description of what the high-priest kings carried out:—

"Save us, O God of all,
And cast thy fear upon all the nations.
Shake thine hand against the strange people,
That they may see Thy power.
As thou has sanctified thyself in us before their eyes,
So sanctify thyself in them before our eyes;
That they may know, even as we know,
That there is none other God but thee.

Subdue the foe, and drive out the enemy.

Gather all the tribes of Jacob,
That they may receive their inheritance as in the days
of old.

Fill Zion with thy majesty,
And thy temple with thy glory.

Hear the prayer of thy servants,
According to thy favour towards thy people.
That all the ends of the earth may know
That thou art the eternal God" (Ecclesiasticus xxxvi.
1–17 in the Hebrew, and xxxiii. 1–13, xxxvi.
16–22, in the Greek).

It will be well here to pause and look back over the history at the attitude taken by the Jews towards the Gentile nations. We have already seen how Second Isaiah had called Israel to be the missionary

of the world, and how Third Isaiah substituted for
that vocation a hope that the Gentiles would be
subjugated under the heel of the Jews. This kind of
thing remained the dominant feeling of the Jews
towards their neighbours, but all along voices were
raised from time to time in favour of a more charit-
able view. The book of Jonah is a satire on the
official attitude of the fifth or fourth century.
Jonah, called to preach to Nineveh, represents the
Jews, who were called to be the world's missionaries;
Jonah tried in vain to avoid his duty, and was
disgusted in the end when the Ninevites repented at
his preaching, and so escaped destruction. Similarly
Ruth was written to counteract the narrow national-
ism, that showed itself in the prohibition of mixed
marriages in the days of Nehemiah and Ezra, Ruth
herself, a member of the hated Moabite race, being
accepted as an Israelite and adopting the faith of
Yahweh. Zechariah ix. 1–10, written about the
time of Alexander the Great, speaks of Aram,
Hamath and Zidon as belonging to Yahweh, and
looks forward to half-castes of Jewish and Philistine
origin being converted from their heathen practices
and being accepted as a clan of Judah. Isaiah
lvi. 1–8, a passage of uncertain date, says that
Babylonian strangers who come to Judaea may be
accepted into all the privileges of Judaism if they
keep the law of the sabbath. A number of passages
in the Psalter breathe the same spirit:—

"All the ends of the earth shall remember and turn unto
the Lord:
And all the kindreds of the nations shall worship before
thee.

For the kingdom is the Lord's:
And He is the ruler over the nations" (Ps. xxii. 27–28).

"O thou that hearest the prayer,
Unto thee shall all flesh come" (Ps. lxv. 2).

"Princes shall come out of Egypt:
Ethiopia shall haste to stretch out her hands unto God"
(Ps. lxviii. 31).

"All nations whom thou hast made shall come and
worship before thee O Lord.
And they shall glorify thy name" (Ps. lxxxvi. 9).

"God reigneth over the nations:
God sitteth upon His holy throne.
The princes of the people are gathered together,
To be the people of the God of Abraham:
For the shields of the earth belong unto God;
He is greatly exalted" (Ps. xlvii. 8–9).

Ben Sira, in the passage already quoted, although
desirous of gathering together the outcasts of Israel,
prays God to shake His fist against the Gentiles and
demonstrate His power. The same attitude is
found a few years later (before 161 B.C.) in the Book
of Enoch:—

"And I saw all the sheep (i.e. the Jews) which had been
left, and all the beasts of the earth and all the birds of the
heaven (the beasts and birds = the Gentiles), falling
down and doing homage to those sheep, making petition
to them, and obeying them in everything" (1 Enoch xc.
30).

"And all that had been destroyed and dispersed (viz.
the sheep, i.e. the Jews), and all the beasts of the field,
and all the birds of the heaven, assembled in that house,
and the Lord of the sheep rejoiced with great joy because
they were all good and had returned to His house"
(1 Enoch xc. 33).

The Book of Jubilees written in the earlier part of the
reign of John Hyrcanus shows the same spirit, only

more definitely declares that God's will for the Gentiles is only to do them evil:—

> "And He sanctified it (i.e. Israel), and gathered it from amongst all the children of men; for there are many nations and many peoples, and all are His, and over all hath He placed spirits to lead them astray from Him. But over Israel He did not appoint any angel or spirit, for He alone is their ruler, and He will preserve them" (Jubilees xv. 31–32).

Fortunately a very different attitude was being taken by others. For the Testament of the Twelve Patriarchs, written at the same time as Jubilees, holds out the brightest hopes for the Gentiles. It has been suggested that this book was written for the benefit of the Israelites, who were being gathered in by Hyrcanus's forcible conversions. Anyhow, what this noble book says is full of hope for all mankind, quite apart from the accident of their birth:—

> "Nevertheless the temple of God shall be in your portion (i.e. in the land of Benjamin), and the last temple shall be more glorious than the first. And the twelve tribes shall be gathered together there, and all the Gentiles" (Testament of Benjamin, ix. 2).

> "And there shall be given unto thee a blessing, and to all thy seed, until the Lord shall visit all the Gentiles in His tender mercies for ever" (Testament of Levi, iv. 4).

The same attitude is still taken up in the following century in the later additions to the book:—

> "But if ye (i.e. Levi's descendants) be darkened through transgression, what, therefore, will all the Gentiles do living in blindness? Yea, ye shall bring a curse upon our race, because the light of the Law which was given for to lighten every man, this ye desire to destroy by teaching commandments contrary to the ordinances of God" (Testament of Levi, xiv. 4).

And right at the end of the first century B.C. the great Rabbi Hillel inculcated love for the Gentiles:—

> "Be of the disciples of Aaron, one that loves peace, that pursues peace, that loves mankind, and brings them nigh to the Torah" (Pirke Aboth, i. 12).

NOTE.

On this chapter read Jonah; Ruth; Zechariah. ix. 1–10; Isaiah lvi. 1–8; Ecclesiasticus xxxvi. 1–17.

Chapter VIII

PHARISEES AND SADDUCEES

Towards the end of the reign of John Hyrcanus, about 105 B.C., we first come across the names of the Pharisees and Sadducees. We must remember that we are still a century and a third away from Gospel times, so we must not too readily assume that the parties in the days of Hyrcanus were the same as their successors in the days of our Lord. We shall not however be very far wrong if we remember that the early Pharisees stood midway between the Hasidim of the days of Antiochus Epiphanes and the Pharisees of the Gospels. The Pharisees were not exactly the descendants of the Hasidim; but they inherited from them their devotion to the Law. One of their early works was the book of Jubilees, written in the reign of Hyrcanus. In this book Genesis was rewritten according to a principle that the Law was not merely a revelation at a certain point of time, but had existed from all eternity written on heavenly tablets and revealed to men by angels.* The Hasidim as far as we know never held such extreme views, though they, like the Pharisaic author of Jubilees, upheld the validity of the Law against the encroachment of Hellenism. Jubilees seems to have believed that the kingdom of God

---

* It is curious to find exactly these same ideas repeating themselves centuries later in Moslem thought about the Qur'an.

would come gradually as people studied the Law more
and more:—

> "And in those days the children shall begin to study the
> laws,
> And to seek the commandments,
> And to return to the path of righteousness.
> And the days shall begin to grow many and increase
> among those children of men
> Till their days draw nigh to one thousand years,
> And to a greater number of years than before was the
> number of the days" (Jubilees xxiii. 26–27).

This education in the Law from infancy is described
by Josephus at the end of the first century A.D. as
follows:—

> "Should any one of our nation be questioned about the
> laws, he would repeat them all more readily than his own
> name. The result, then, of our thorough grounding in
> the laws from the time when we first had any sensations
> whatever, is that we have them as it were engraven on
> our souls" (Josephus, *Apion*, ii. 18).

The Pharisees, for all their adherence to the Law,
accepted the new doctrine of the resurrection, and the
development of thought about angels and the other
world. They were more definitely a party than the
Hasidim, and their strength lay in their scribes under
whose care there gradually grew up a collection of
decisions on conduct and doctrine.

The Sadducees were the descendants of the
Hellenisers of the time of Antiochus Epiphanes, and
opposed the Pharisees as the Hellenisers had
opposed the Hasidim. But the Sadducees too had
changed, for there was now no more thought of
introducing Greek customs or idolatry. The First
Book of Maccabees is the work of a Sadducee, and

his heroes are not the Hasidim but the Maccabean leaders. Religion was not exactly dead with the Sadducees, but was pushed far away out of touch with daily life. The impersonal word "Heaven" seemed to them the most appropriate way of referring to God. They were to be found mostly among the priests. The due performance of the temple ritual according to the Pentateuch was all that could be expected of them. They were equally averse to the doctrines and practice developed by the Pharisees, and to the religion of the heart taught by the Old Testament prophets.

We saw in the early days of the Maccabean movement that the Hasidim only gave their support to the Maccabees so long as they were fighting purely for spiritual ends. One could not imagine the Maccabees calling themselves Hasidim; but they might be included within the term "Pharisees," for the Pharisees never had that detachment from the world that had marked the Hasidim. There was, it is true, another offshoot of the Hasidim which developed to an extreme that very characteristic of aloofness from the world: they were called Essenes, and existed right up to New Testament times. They had all their possessions in common, and lived a sober and somewhat ascetic life; they did not marry, but kept up their numbers by adopting children. They did not offer sacrifices in the temple, but observed lustrations of their own. It is doubtful whether their peculiar manner of life and doctrine had much influence on the Jews generally.

The Pharisees were attached to the side of the Maccabean rulers till the later years of John

Hyrcanus; but eventually, owing no doubt to his increasingly worldly policy, a cleavage took place, and Hyrcanus declared himself a Sadducee. The book known as the Testament of the Twelve Patriarchs was written by a Pharisee during the reign of John Hyrcanus before he joined the Sadducees. There is a fine passage on forgiveness which stands as a monument of what Pharisaism was at its best:—

> "Love ye one another from the heart; and if a man sin against thee, speak peaceably to him, and in thy soul hold not guile; and if he repent and confess forgive him. But if he deny it, do not get into a passion with him, lest catching the poison from thee he take to swearing, and so thou sin doubly. And though he deny it and yet have a sense of shame when reproved, give over reproving him. For he who denieth may repent so as not again to wrong thee; yea, he may also honour thee, and be at peace with thee. And if he be shameless and persist in his wrong-doing, even so forgive him from the heart, and leave to God the avenging" (Testament of Gad, vi. 3–7).

A similar ethical note is found earlier in Ecclesiasticus ii. 4–5:—

> "Accept whatsoever is brought upon thee,
>   And be longsuffering when thou passest into humiliation.
> For gold is tried in the fire,
>   And acceptable men in the furnace of affliction."

A much later work, the Slavonic Enoch, composed in the first half of the first century A.D., inculcates a similar bearing under affliction in view of the coming judgment:—

> "Now therefore, my children, in patience and meekness spend the number of your days, that you inherit endless life. Endure for the sake of the Lord every wound, every injury, every evil word and attack. If ill-requitals befall

you, return them not either to neighbour or enemy, because the Lord will return them for you and be your avenger on the day of great judgment, that there be no avenging here among men. . . . And every grievous and cruel yoke that come upon you, bear all for the sake of the Lord, and thus you will find your reward in the day of judgment." (2 Enoch l. 2–4, li. 3).

In keeping with their descent from the Hasidim the Pharisees developed that kind of literature which we call Apocalyptic, the chief representative of which was the Book of Daniel, practically the only Apocalyptic book which was commonly known until fairly recent times. In fact, with their adherence to the Torah as the final expression of God's will, it was no longer possible to write as the prophets had written; and yet the Holy Spirit working within them forced them to utterance. And the result was this extraordinary literature in which ancient worthies are represented as having visions of the distant future. Pessimism as to the present world-order, and hope for a completely fresh start in another world, are the prevailing notes of Apocalyptic. The Messiah of the Prophets, and the Messianic kingdom, naturally occupied a place in such schemes, and the resurrection, the judgment, heaven and hell, are recurrent themes. The term "Son of Man" as a Messianic title appears first in Daniel vii. 13–14:—

"I saw in the night visions, and, behold, there came with the clouds of heaven one like unto a son of man, and he came even to the ancient of days, and they brought him near before Him. And there was given him dominion, and glory, and a kingdom, that all the peoples, nations, and languages should serve him: his dominion is an ever-lasting dominion, which shall not pass away, and his kingdom that which shall not be destroyed."

We have not much to guide us as to the interpretation of the Son of Man in this passage, but it is probable that we should regard this figure in two aspects, as an individual and also as a personification of the nation, just as we found earlier in the case of the Messiah (see page 17). In the earliest part of the book of Enoch, written before 161 B.C., the Messiah comes after the judgment but does not play any very conspicuous part except as the first of mankind to return to the immortality and bliss of the Garden of Eden. In the Prophets the Messiah had always been of David's royal line, i.e. of the house of Judah, but while the Pharisees trusted in the Maccabean princes they looked for a Messiah of the house of Levi. This is what we find in the Testament of the Twelve Patriarchs. But in other places in the same book the Messiah is expected to come from Judah, and it is commonly supposed that such passages are later interpolations reflecting the changed views of the Pharisees after Hyrcanus had left them and given his favour to the Sadducees:—

"Then shall the Lord raise up a new priest,
  And to him all the words of the Lord shall be revealed;
  And he shall execute a righteous judgment upon the
      earth for a multitude of days.
  And his star shall arise in heaven as of a king,
  Lighting up the light of knowledge as the sun the day,
  And he shall be magnified in the world.

              .   .   .   .

  The heavens shall be open,
  And from the temple of glory shall come upon him
      sanctification,
  With the Father's voice as from Abraham to Isaac.
  And the glory of the Most High shall be uttered over him,

And the spirit of understanding and sanctification shall
    rest upon him.
For he shall give the majesty of the Lord to his sons in
    truth for evermore;
And there shall none succeed him for all generations for
    ever.
And in his priesthood the Gentiles shall be multiplied
    in knowledge upon the earth,
And enlightened through the grace of the Lord:
In his priesthood shall sin come to an end,
And the lawless shall cease to do evil" (Testament
    of Levi, xviii. 2–9).

"With the Father's voice as from Abraham to
Isaac" must mean that God would speak to the
Messiah of his sacrificial death, for the only word
that Abraham is recorded to have said to Isaac is,
"God will provide Himself with a lamb for a burnt
offering, my son" (Gen. xxii. 8). Thus we see in
this passage one of the very few identifications of the
Messiah with the Suffering Servant. It is not
surprising that Christians (who alone preserved the
text of the book, and inserted numerous additions)
took this passage as referring to our Lord's baptism,
and added the words "in the water" after the line
"And the spirit of understanding and sanctification
shall rest upon him." The addition is found in all
except one Greek manuscript.

Another closely parallel passage, which has
several identical clauses, makes the Messiah spring
from Judah rather than from Levi:—

"And after these things shall a star arise to you from
    Jacob in peace,
And a man shall arise from my seed like the sun of
    righteousness,
Walking with the sons of men in meekness and
    righteousness;

And no sin shall be found in him.
And the heavens shall be open unto him,
To pour out the spirit, even the blessing of the holy
Father;
And he shall pour out the spirit of grace upon you;
And ye shall be unto him sons in truth,
And ye shall walk in his commandments first and last"
(Testament of Judah xxiv. 1-3).

Some modern scholars think that the author of the Testaments actually conceived of two Messiahs, one from Levi and one from Judah, and in this way interpret the following passage:*

"And now, my children, I command you, love Levi, that he may abide, and exalt not yourselves against him, lest ye be utterly destroyed. For to me the Lord gave the kingdom, and to him the priesthood, and He set the kingdom beneath the priesthood. To me He gave the things upon the earth; to him the things in the heavens. As the heaven is higher than the earth, so is the priesthood of God higher than the earthly kingdom, unless it falls away through sin from the Lord and is dominated by the earthly kingdom. For the angel of the Lord said unto me: The Lord chose him rather than thee, to draw near to Him, and to eat of His table and to offer Him the first-fruits of the choice things of the sons of Israel; but thou shalt be king of Jacob" (Testament of Judah, xxi. 1-5).

A fuller description of the Messiah is found in that part of Enoch which dates from the first half of the first century B.C. Here we find the Messiah represented as judge, as sinless, as revealer of heavenly secrets, and as a pre-existent being:—

"On that day mine Elect One shall sit on the throne of glory,
And shall try their works,
And their places of rest shall be innumerable.

* G. R. Beasley-Murray in *The Evangelical Quarterly* for July, 1947.

Then will I cause mine Elect One to dwell among them.
And I will transform the heaven and make it an eternal
    blessing and light:
And I will transform the earth and make it a blessing:
And I will cause mine elect ones to dwell upon it:
But the sinners and evil doers shall not set foot thereon"
    (1 Enoch xlv. 3–5).

"And there I saw One who had a head of days,
And His head was white like wool,
And with Him was another being whose countenance had
    the appearance of a man,
And his face was full of graciousness like one of the
    holy angels.

        .   .   .   .

This is the Son of Man who hath righteousness,
With whom dwelleth righteousness,
And who revealeth all the treasures of that which is
    hidden,
Because the Lord of Spirits hath chosen him" (1 Enoch
    xlvi. 1, 3).

"And at that hour the Son of Man was named
In the presence of the Lord of Spirits,
And his name before the Head of Days.
Yea, before the sun and the signs were created,
Before the stars of the heaven were made,
His name was named before the Lord of Spirits.
He shall be a staff to the righteous whereon to stay
    themselves and not fall,
And he shall be the light of the Gentiles,
And the hope of those that are troubled of heart.
All who dwell on the earth shall fall down and worship
    before him,
And will praise and bless and celebrate with song the
    Lord of Spirits.
And for this reason hath he been chosen and hidden
    before Him,
Before the creation of the world and for evermore"
    (1 Enoch xlviii. 2–6).

The speaker in Enoch xlviii. 1, who saw God and the
Son of Man, was Enoch, the ancient worthy of
Gen. v. 21-24, of the sixth generation from Adam,
who "walked with God, and he was not, for God
took him." He is mentioned in Ecclesiasticus
xliv. 16 and xlix. 14 as the only one who was taken
up from the earth because he pleased God. Towards
the end of the Book of Enoch, in a passage that is
probably intended as the climax of the book, Enoch
is told that he is himself the Son of Man:—

"And he (the angel) came to me (Enoch) and greeted me
> with his voice, and said unto me,
'Thou art the Son of Man who art born unto righteous-
> ness,
And righteousness abides over thee,
And the righteousness of the Head of Days forsakes
> thee not.'
And he said unto me:
'He proclaims unto thee peace in the name of the world
> to come;
For from hence has proceeded peace since the creation
> of the world,
And so shall it be unto thee for ever and for ever and
> ever.
And all shall walk in thy ways since righteousness
> never forsaketh thee:
With thee will be their dwelling-places, and with thee
> their heritage,
And they shall not be separated from thee for ever and
> ever and ever.
And so shall there be length of days with that Son of Man,
And the righteous shall have peace and an upright way
In the name of the Lord of spirits for ever and ever'"
> (1 Enoch lxxi. 14–17).

The statement in 1 Enoch xlviii. 2 that the Son
of Man was named before the creation presumably

meant that he existed before the creation. The idea that the Son of Man existed before his advent is carried further in 1 Enoch lxxi. 14 by his being identified in some sense with the ancient Enoch. This identification is so surprising that R. H. Charles thought it must have been due to textual corruption, and therefore in his translation he emended the text to read *"This is* the Son of Man" instead of *"Thou art* the Son of Man," etc. But later scholarship has confirmed the existence of a belief that the Son of Man or Messiah was to be a return of Enoch to earth, somewhat like the belief found in the Gospels that John the Baptist was a reincarnation of Elijah. Now, just as it is natural for us to express such ideas by the use of the word "reincarnation," so the identification of the Son of Man with the perfect man Enoch would appear to the early Christians as a foreshadowing of the incarnation of Christ; while the dwelling of the righteous with him, sharing his righteousness, would seem to be a foretaste of the Christian doctrine of life in union with Christ. Such a Christian interpretation seems to have been known to later Jews, for one place in the Talmud* forbids the worship of Metatron or the "Lesser Yahweh" as a mediator between God and Israel, and this Metatron is elsewhere identified with the translated Enoch.

A few year later, about the middle of the first century B.C., the Psalms of Solomon give a further picture of the Messiah, the main feature of the picture being a reign of peace free from the distractions of enemies without and sin within:—

* Babylonian Talmud, Sanhedrin 38b.

16173

"Behold O Lord, and raise up unto them their king, the
  son of David,
At the time in which thou seest, O God, that he may
  reign over Israel thy servant.
And gird him with strength that he may shatter
  unrighteous rulers,
And that he may purge Jerusalem from nations that
  trample her down to destruction.

     .   .   .   .

And he (shall be) a righteous king, taught of God, over
  them,
And there shall be no unrighteousness in his days in
  their midst,
For all shall be holy and their king the anointed (of)
  the Lord.
For he shall not put his trust in horse and rider and bow.

     .   .   .   .

The Lord Himself is his King, the hope of him that is
  mighty through his hope in God.

     .   .   .   .

For God will make him mighty by means of (His) holy
  spirit,
And by means of the spirit of understanding, with
  strength and righteousness.

     .   .   .   .

May the Lord hasten His mercy upon Israel!
May He deliver us from the uncleanness of unholy
  enemies!
The Lord Himself is our King for ever and ever"
  (Ps. Sol. xvii. 23–51).

A little later, between A.D. 7 and 30, too early to
have been influenced by Christianity, we have a
picture of the Messianic kingdom as affecting the
whole world order:—

"And then His kingdom shall appear throughout all His
  creation,
And then Satan shall be no more,

And sorrow shall depart with him.
Then the hands of the angel shall be filled
Who has been appointed chief,
And he shall forthwith avenge them of their enemies.
For the heavenly One shall arise from His royal throne,
And He will go forth from His holy habitation
With indignation and wrath on account of His sons.
And the earth shall tremble: to its confines shall it be
    shaken:
And the high mountains shall be made low
And the hills shall be shaken and fall.
And the horns of the sun shall be broken and he shall be
    turned into darkness;
And the moon shall not give her light, and be turned
    wholly into blood.
And the circle of the stars shall be disturbed.
And the sea shall retire into the abyss,
And the fountains of water shall fail,
And the rivers shall dry up.
For the Most High will arise, the eternal God alone,
And He will appear to punish the Gentiles,
And He will destroy all their idols.
Then thou, O Israel, shalt be happy,
And thou shalt mount upon the necks and wings of the
    eagle,
And they shall be ended.
And God will exalt thee,
And He will cause thee to approach to the heaven of the
    stars,
In the place of their habitation.
And thou shalt look from on high and shalt see thine
    enemies in Gehenna,
And thou shalt recognise them and rejoice,
And thou shalt give thanks and confess thy Creator."
    (Assumption of Moses x. 1–10).

As a sequel to these pre-Christian hopes of the
Messianic kingdom, we may add one from what
Dr. Charles called "the last noble utterance of

Judaism before it plunged into the dark and oppressive years that followed the destruction of Jerusalem." This was the Apocalypse of Baruch, written in the second half of the first century A.D.:—

> "And it shall come to pass, when He has brought low
>   everything that is in the world,
> And has sat down in peace for the age on the throne of
>   His kingdom,
> That joy shall then be revealed,
> And rest shall appear.
> And then healing shall descend in dew,
> And disease shall withdraw,
> And anxiety and anguish and lamentation pass from
>   amongst men,
> And gladness proceed through the whole earth.
> And no one shall again die untimely,
> Nor shall any adversity suddenly befall.
> And judgments and revilings and contentions and
>   revenges,
> And blood and passions and envy and hatred,
> And whatsoever things are like these shall go into
>   condemnation when they are removed.
> For it is these very things which have filled this world
>   with evils,
> And on account of these the life of man has been greatly
>   troubled.
> And wild beasts shall come from the forest and minister
>   unto men,
> And asps and dragons shall come forth from their holes
>   to submit themselves to a little child.
> And women shall no longer then have pain when they
>   bear,
> Nor shall they suffer torment when they yield the fruit
>   of the womb." (2 Baruch lxxiii. 1–7).

There seems to have been a diversity of opinion about the resurrection, whether it would be a resurrection of the body or only of the soul. Jubilees towards the end of the second century thought of the resurrection of the soul only:—

> "And the righteous shall see and be thankful,
> And rejoice with joy for ever and ever,
> And shall see all their judgments and all their curses on their enemies.
> And their bones shall rest in the earth,
> And their spirits shall have much joy" (Jubilees xxiii. 30–31).

Half a century or so later Enoch speaks equally definitely of resurrection of the body:—

> "And in those days shall the earth also give back that which has been entrusted to it,
> And She'ol also shall give back that which it has received,
> And hell shall give back that which it owes"
>
> (1 Enoch li. 1).

Towards the end of the first century B.C. the book of the Wisdom of Solomon thinks rather of the immortality of the soul than of resurrection. Possibly this may be due to the influence of Greek thought:—

> "But the souls of the righteous are in the hand of God,
> And no torment shall touch them.
> In the eyes of the foolish they seemed to have died;
> And their departure was accounted to be their hurt,
> And their journeying away from us to be their ruin:
> But they are in peace.
> For even if in the sight of men they be punished,
> Their hope is full of immortality." (Wisdom iii. 1–4).

But this view of immortality did not supersede the belief in the resurrection of the body, which is finely

expressed in the Sibylline Oracles, composed about
80 A.D.:—

"But when now all things shall have been reduced
   To dust and ashes, and God shall have calmed
   The fire unspeakable which He lit up,
   The bones and ashes of men God Himself
   Again will fashion, and He will again
   Raise mortals up, even as they were before.
   And then shall be the judgment, at which God
   Himself as judge shall judge the world again;
   And all who sinned with impious hearts, even them
   Shall He again hide under mounds of earth,
   Dark Tartarus and Stygian Gehenna.
   But all who shall be pious shall again
   Live on the earth and shall inherit there
   The great immortal God's unwasting bliss,
   God giving spirit, life and joy to them
   The pious; and they all shall see themselves
   Beholding the sun's sweet and cheering light.
   Oh happy on the earth shall be that man." (Sib. Or. iv.
      179–192).*

Josephus distinguished the three parties of the
Jews by their opinion on the question of free-will
and predestination.   He said that the Essenes
ascribed all things to God, or Fate, while the
Sadducees went to the opposite extreme, taking
away Fate entirely and supposing that God is not
concerned in our doing or not doing what is evil.
The Pharisees, he said, occupied an intermediate
position, ascribing everything to Fate and to God,
and yet asserting that right or wrong action was in
the power of men; or in other words that actions are
liable to Fate, but not caused by Fate (Josephus,
Ant. xiii. v. 9, xviii. i. 3–5, War ii. viii. 14).   This

* From the translation by M. S. Terry.

clear-cut division does not seem quite to tally with our evidence. It is true that the subject was much debated, but there was no unanimity on the subject among the Pharisees. Ben Sira had attributed the origin of sin to man's nature and not to God:—

"From a woman was the beginning of sin;
  And because of her we all die"
    (Ecclesiasticus xxv. 24).

"Say not, 'From God is my transgression,'
  For that which He hateth made He not" (Ecclesiasticus xv. 11).

"God created man from the beginning,
  And placed him in the hand of his *yetzer* (i.e. evil tendency, or nature)" (Ecclesiasticus xv. 14).

But a later interpolator added after the first line of verse 14 the words, "and delivered him into the hand of him that spoileth him." This suggestion of an extraneous evil power is found in the Book of Noah, a work composed probably in the first half of the second century B.C. and known to us only through selections which are found in Enoch and Jubilees. The Book of Noah taught that the marriage of heavenly beings with the daughters of men (Gen. vi. 2), was the cause of sin entering the world. With this agrees 1 Enoch lxix. 11, written in the first half of the first century B.C.:—

"For men were created exactly like the angels, to the intent that they should continue pure and righteous, and death, which destroys everything, could not have taken hold of them; but through this their knowledge (imparted by the evil angels) they are perishing."

But another part of Enoch, written at the same

time as the piece just quoted, seeks the origin of sin within the heart of man:—

"Sin hath not been sent upon the earth,
But man of himself hath created it,
And under a great curse shall they fall who commit it"
(1 Enoch xcviii. 4).

Finally towards the end of the first century the blame is put on the Devil:—

"Because God created man for incorruption,
And made him an image of His own proper being;
But by the envy of the devil death entered into the world,
And they that belong to his realm experience it"
(Wisdom ii. 23–24).

Of the attitude of the Sadducees on the question we have not much information, but the Pharisaic interpolator of Ecclesiasticus, attacking the Sadducean position, attributes to them a crass belief in free-will, which agrees well enough with the testimony of Josephus:—

"Better inexorable persistence in seeking the Lord,
Than a masterless charioteer of his own life" (Ecclesiasticus xx. 31, Codex 248).

The Apocalyptic literature is so extensive that it has only been possible to give a few quotations to show the sort of thoughts that were occupying the minds of the Jews in the last two centuries B.C., but it will be realised how greatly a knowledge of this literature helps one to understand the religious background of the Gospels.

NOTE.

On this chapter read Wisdom i–iii. 9.

Chapter IX

THE KING OF THE JEWS

105–4 B.C.

ARISTOBULUS, son of John Hyrcanus, the first of the Maccabean house to adopt the title of king, reigned but one year, when he was succeeded about 105 B.C. by his brother Alexander Jannaeus, who reigned as king and high priest for close on thirty years. The Hasidim of the early days, who had distrusted the political aims of the Maccabean leaders, had rightly gauged the effect of a rule in which religion was relegated to the second place; and their successors, the Pharisees under Jannaeus, saw to their sorrow the dreadful fruitage of Maccabean rule and tyranny. Jannaeus spent his time in waging savage warfare for the extension of his kingdom. It was not without reason that he continued the anti-Pharisaic policy of his father, for he had no mind to uphold the sanctity of religion, though, for the sake of power, he clung to the office of the high-priesthood. The desecration of the holy office was too much for the Pharisees and the other Jews to whom religion was still a real thing, and on one occasion the worshippers in their wrath pelted the man with lemons as he officiated at the Feast of Tabernacles. The insult was paid for in blood; but worse things were yet to follow. For the Jews, whose hatred of their king was rising, took advantage of a moment when he was being worsted in an encounter with the Nabataean Arabs, now a powerful kingdom settled in the old land of Edom, south of the Dead Sea. They sought the aid of a Syrian king against Jannaeus, and would have defeated him, but at the last moment the courage of many of them failed for fear of subjugation once more to the power of Antioch. Jannaeus came out victorious, and the awful sight was seen in Jerusalem of eight hundred Pharisees crucified by the order of their high priest. No wonder that the wrath of the Pharisees was stirred up, not only against the high priest, but also against his Sudducean supporters:—

> "Woe to you, ye rich, for ye have trusted in your riches,
>   And from your riches shall ye depart,
>   Because ye have not remembered the Most High in the
>   days of your riches.
>   Ye have committed blasphemy and unrighteousness,
>   And have become ready for the day of slaughter,
>   And the day of darkness and the day of the great
>   judgment" (1 Enoch xciv. 8–9).

After the death of Jannaeus the Pharisees had their chance for the next nine years, during which the country was ruled by his widow Alexandra. She ruled with a firm hand, but without the thirst for aggressive warfare that had possessed her husband. For some reason she gave her favour to the Pharisees, and it was now the turn of the Sadducees to know the terror of the assassin's dagger. The Pharisees were no doubt taking literally the prophecy uttered in the days of their own distress:—

> "Be hopeful, ye righteous; for suddenly shall the sinners
>   perish before you,
>   And ye shall have lordship over them according to your
>   desires" (1 Enoch xcvi. 1).

Alexandra of course could not be high priest, so she

had appointed her son Hyrcanus, a weak man, who could only hold office as the tool of another. As soon as Queen Alexandra died the kingship and high-priesthood were seized by a stronger son Aristobulus. But conditions abroad were not to leave Judaea in peace. The Nabataeans were still strong, but the centre of interest now rested in their neighbours the Idumaeans, who lived south of Judah, or rather in a single man among them named Antipater. Outwardly a Jew, he obviously shared little if any religious convictions with the Jews, and his policy, and that of the whole Herodian house, who followed him, was simply personal aggrandisement. Antipater found Hyrcanus a useful tool, and with the help of the Nabataeans he proceeded to restore Hyrcanus to the Jewish throne. When his plan was nearly consummated a new power suddenly appeared as the arbiter of Judaea's destinies. For years the influence of Rome had been feared, like the rum-blings of a distant thunderstorm; but the arrival in Syria of a general sent by Pompey, was like the bursting of the storm. Now the contending parties in Judaea desisted from fighting one another, and each tried by guile and bribes to win the favour of Pompey. Was it folly on the part of Aristobulus, or some spark of patriotism, which led him, after failing to win the conqueror by bribes, to attempt to bar the way to his advance? Was it utter lack of patriot-ism, or the wisdom that knew better than resist an irresistible force, which led Antipater to welcome Pompey to the city? Anyhow, we have the strange sight of the Roman forces, masters of the city by the favour of Antipater and his party, besieging

Aristobulus and his party in the temple.   Finally on
the Day of Atonement 63 B.C. the temple was taken.
The priests did not try to escape, but continued their
offerings at the altar till they were slain.   Aristobulus and thousands of Jews were taken to Rome,
the former to mark the victor's triumph, the latter
to be sold as slaves.   These slaves were the main
body which gave rise to the large number of Jews
whom we find in Rome in the days of the Apostles.
For slaves who refused under any circumstances to
work one day in seven were little use to Roman
masters, and most of them were soon given their
freedom.   The Psalms of Solomon, written at this
time, show the horror with which the Jews saw the
invasion of Pompey; but the author cannot help
regarding the desecration as a just judgment of
God on Israel for the sins of the nation.

> "He (God) brought him that is from the end of the earth,
>   that smiteth mightily;
> He decreed war against Jerusalem, and against her land.
> The princes of the land went to meet him with joy: they
>   said unto him:
> Blessed by thy way!   Come ye, enter ye with peace.
> They made the rough ways even, before his entering in;
> They opened the gates to Jerusalem, they crowned its
>   walls.   .   .   .   .
>
> He captured her fortresses and the wall of Jerusalem;
> For God Himself led him in safety, while they
>   wandered" (Ps. Sol. viii. 16–21).

> "When the sinner waxed proud, with a battering ram he
>   cast down fortified walls,
> And thou didst not restrain him.
> Alien nations ascended thine altar,
> They trampled it proudly with their sandals" (Ps. Sol.
>   ii. 1–2).

"The lawless one laid waste our land so that none
    inhabited it;
They destroyed young and old and their children
    together.
In the heat of his anger he sent them away unto the
    west,
And he exposed the rulers of the land unsparingly to
    derision" (Ps. Sol. xvii. 13).

The Romans left Hyrcanus as high priest in Jerusalem, and Antipater was still the power behind him.
The internal troubles of the Roman state forced the
Roman rulers to act severely towards the Jews, and
the result was that Jewish territory was once more
reduced to narrow limits. A little later, however,
Antipater used the forces at his command to help
Caesar at a critical juncture, and Caesar's consequent
friendship to Antipater gave back to the Jews some
of their lost territory. The constant changes of
power in Rome kept Antipater busy with intrigues,
seeking the favour of one new master after another;
and when Antipater was poisoned in 43 B.C., his son
Herod carried on the same skilful and unscrupulous
intrigues. A temporary success of the Parthians
against the Romans resulted in the loss by Hyrcanus
of the high-priesthood and the flight of Herod. But
Herod was not outwitted; for with a determination
that compels our admiration he reached Rome at
a time of the year when sailing was well-nigh impossible, got recognized as king of the Jews, and then
hastened back to fight for his kingdom. The
Parthians had appointed as high priest Antigonus,
son of the Aristobulus who had opposed Pompey.
With the help of the Romans, Herod fought against
Antigonus, and besieged and captured Jerusalem.

Antigonus, the last of the Maccabean princes, was taken prisoner and beheaded in 37 B.C. All that remained of the family of the Maccabees were exterminated by Herod, except Mariamne whom he made his wife. Herod's long reign of thirty-three years was a time of material prosperity. He extended the borders of Israel by the favour of Octavianus Caesar (later known as Augustus); new cities were built; and magnificent buildings were erected, including a new temple to replace the temple of Zerubbabel. But spiritually they were dark days, on which we do not care to dwell. From the beginning of his reign when he put to death forty-five of the chief Sadducean leaders, to the end when he executed three of his own sons, it is a tale of cruelty, and there is little to admire in the personal character of this foreign ruler. It is not surprising that the best hopes of the Jews in those days, which we find reflected in the Psalms of Solomon, centred on a kingdom in which peace and righteousness should reign (see p. 101). For the troubles of those days only threw into stronger relief the bright hopes of those who had visions of the future. As we look back we seem to stand at the end of things. Prophecy had long ago done its best, and had ceased. Legalism had performed its task of creating a framework for the outward religious life of the nation; its later development was like extraneous carvings added to ancient architecture, which while giving more complexity, add nothing to the pristine dignity. The old problems of free-will and predestination, and of the origin of evil, had been canvassed till there was nothing more to be said, and no solution had been found.   Apocalyptic had blossomed and filled men's hearts with hopes, but the variety and indefiniteness of the visions left people just hoping, yet scarcely knowing what they were hoping for.   When Herod the king, at the end of his reign, put the question to the chief priests and scribes where the Messiah was to be born, it was not to the Apocalyptic literature, but to the book of the Prophets that they turned for an answer (Matt. ii. 4–6).   There were many in those days who were looking for the redemption of Jerusalem.   Some such people were guided by an aged woman of the tribe of Asher— probably a child of parents brought back into the Jewish fold by John Hyrcanus or Aristobulus—to look for that redemption in the infant Jesus (Luke ii. 36–38).   For in the later years of Herod there had been born at Bethlehem the Child who fulfilled the highest hopes of prophets and psalmists and apocalyptists—the Saviour of the world.

This last chapter began with Aristobulus, the first of the Maccabean family to claim the title of king of the Jews; it continued with the story of the strange rise to power of Herod the Great till he was proclaimed king of the Jews by the Roman Emperor; it ends with the birth of One of the house of David, who was hailed king of the Jews in His cradle by sages from the east, who bore the title of King of the Jews over His cross, and who is worshipped to-day as king both of Jews and Gentiles in every land, and whose kingdom shall have no end.

General Index

Index of Scripture
and Other Passages